G000230626

HISTORIC SUSSEX

A Guide Book

by

CHRIS HARE

23355

Rye Road, Hastings, East Sussex, TN35 5DN

First published in 1998 by Southern Heritage Books
35, Salvington Hill, Worthing, West Sussex. BN13 3BB

Text: Christopher A Hare

ISBN 0-9527097-2-4

British Library Cataloguing in Publication Data.
A Catalogue record for this book is available from the
British Library.

All rights reserved. No part of this publication may be
reproduced, stored in a retrieval system, or transmitted
in any way or by any means, electronic, mechanical,
photocopying, recording or otherwise, without the prior
permission of the publishers.

Printed by the Print Unit, The Tannery, Westgate, Chichester.

CONTENTS

To Ann with love

FOREWORD

Chris Hare is one of the newer generation of Sussex authors and brings a freshness of approach into an old subject. His Historic Sussex – a guide book deals comprehensibly not only with events of widespread significance but also with the intimate matters of a more personal nature. Documentary and anecdotal accounts are given equal attention and the result is a history of Sussex taken in the round.

The fruits of his tireless researches are written in such a way as to lead the reader on, as any well-told story should, from one important event to the next, but never losing sight of the humble happenings which add substance and warmth to the cold, dry bones of formal history. Quotes from the Anglo-Saxon Chronicle and numerous other contemporary writings ensure that the Saxon era, the Norman Conquest, the Civil War and so on are vividly brought to life with real flesh and blood taking part. We are told of the 'Swing Riots' in the 1830's, but we also learn why, while the nefarious 'Captain Swing' was cutting a swathe of violence and destruction across the Weald in protest against the introduction of the threshing machine, the farm labourers of Rottingdean on the coast were working under a benign master, who ensured that the introduction of the new machines did not lead to the unemployment and poverty seen elsewhere in the county. At Rottingdean the labourers sang in praise of the threshing machine –

> " The man who made her he made her so well
> He made every cog and wheel to tell.
> The big wheel runs and the little 'en hums
> And the feeder he sits above the drums,
> Singing, Rumble-dum-dairy, flare up Mary,
> Make her old table shine."

I do not agree with Henry Ford's blunt assertion that history is bunk. Knowledge of what we are broadens our view of what we are, and the train of events which has led us to the present day carries hints, even warnings, of what we may expect in the future. In any case it is fascinating to be taken back in time to the distant days when that ancient yew tree in the corner of the churchyard was a mere sapling. This is a history of the county told in an interesting and diverting manner.

Bob Copper
Peacehaven

ACKNOWLEDGMENTS

The author would like to thank West Sussex County Library Service for permission to reproduce engravings and photographs in their possession. All those illustrations that come from the county collection appear with 'WSCC' in parenthesis. Particular thanks are due to Martin Hayes, Robin Knibb and Esme Evans at Worthing Library for their help and advice.

Those illustrations which appear with 'FG' in parenthesis were drawn by Frederick Griggs in 1903 and originally appeared in E V Lucas' 'Highways and Byways in Sussex', published in 1904. The photograph of Bailiffscourt which is reproduced on page 36 appears courtesy of Mr. Adge Roberts of East Preston. All other illustrations are copied from originals held by the author.

The author would like to thank Dr. Peter Brandon, Bob Copper, Jacqueline Simpson and Tony Wales for reading the manuscript of this book, and for making helpful and important comments and criticisms. The author is particularly grateful to Bob Copper for agreeing to write the Foreword. Thanks are due to Shaun Payne for information regarding the life of Arthur Beckett. Finally, the author would like to thank Kathryn Haigh for her diligent proof-reading, and Steve Rendle at the Print Unit for his patience.

HOW TO USE THIS BOOK

In writing this book my aim has been to combine a guide or gazetteer to Sussex with a history of the county. I have divided Sussex up into ten areas and provide a brief history and description of each of their most historic towns and villages.

As well as describing the salient events in the history of Sussex, I have included aspects of local history which other guide books have overlooked. My intention has been to tell the history of people rather than of buildings. When I mention specific buildings and historic places, I do so in order to tell the story of the occupants and the part they played in the history of Sussex.

Four of the chapters concern themes, viz. – Saxon and Norman Heritage, The Reformation, The Civil War, Crime and Punishment and describe the crucial moments in Sussex history. You will notice that together they form a considerable proportion of this book, and you may like to read these chapters first, as they set the historical backdrop of every town and village in Sussex. Throughout the 'gazetteer' section of the book I have made frequent references to relevant pages in the 'themed' chapters, for your information.

In the book, I have 'boiled-down' many worthy tomes, to give what I hope is an accurate and lively summary of current thinking on these important topics. A full bibliography appears for each 'themed' chapter at the end of the book. A bibliography, in alphabetical order, also appears for the major towns and villages. Where possible, I have sought to list books currently in publication. Where books are out of print, I have ensured that copies are available in the local studies collection at Worthing Library.

One important aspect of this book is the inclusion of earlier writings concerning Sussex and its history. Throughout the book you will find quotations from a number of authors, whose descriptions and commentaries are of both literary as well as historical merit. It is worth briefly 'introducing' these particular Sussex writers to you now.

Sussex writers

Arthur Beckett (1872-1943) was co-founder of 'Beckett Newspapers', founding President of the Society of Sussex Downsmen, and founding editor of the Sussex County Magazine. He was a great chronicler of local history and historical anecdotes. To the modern reader, Beckett's censorious attitude towards those he insisted on referring to as the 'peasantry' appears highly patronising. Beckett was a middle class Edwardian gentleman and consequently displayed the prejudices of his times. Yet, peel away the bluster and there is much to commend in Beckett's writing, which records a Sussex long since gone. 'The Spirit of the Downs', published in 1909, was his most successful book.

Hilaire Belloc (1870-1953) was a pugnacious defender of Sussex and its traditions. He lived as a boy at Slindon, and in later life at Shipley. His love of controversy and in particular his championing of a medieval form of Roman-Catholicism, brought him into conflict with modern ideas and attitudes. Belloc, who viewed much of modern life as absurd, took great delight in the stubborn ruralism which still lingered in parts of this county up until the Second World War. One of his most famous books, 'The Four Men', published in 1911, concerns the journey, discussions and arguments of four companions travelling across Sussex on foot, from east to west. The 'four men' have been seen as the four aspects of Belloc's own multi-faceted personality.

Tickner Edwardes (1865-1944) lived a remarkable and varied life. He forsook the family business for a career in journalism. Around 1897 he moved to Burpham, and was to die there nearly half a century later. As well as a writer, he was also a respected bee-keeper, and wrote several books on the subject. Despite being nearly fifty in 1914, he enlisted into the British Army, and served throughout the conflict. After the War, he trained for the priesthood, and in 1927 succeeded in becoming vicar of his beloved Burpham. 'Lift Luck on Southern Roads', published in 1910, is one of his most readable and engaging books.

Augustus Hare (1834-1903) was a prolific travel writer, whose unfinished autobiography was reputed to be the longest ever written in the English language. Hare was brought up by his uncle, the Rector of Hurstmonceux. He was cruelly treated by Uncle Julius and Aunt Maria, who regularly flogged him and deprived him of all childish pleasures. As an adult Hare tried to erase this traumatic upbringing by immersing himself in the pleasures of travel and the collection of art and antiques. He lived at Ore, near Hastings. He wrote a guide to the county, called simply 'Sussex'.

W. H. Hudson (1841-1922) spent his formative years in Argentina and later wrote extensively about the people and natural history of South America. He was an admirer of Richard Jefferies, although the two men never met. Hudson's book, 'Nature in Downland', published in 1899, was written in Jefferies' old house at Goring, and can be regarded as a literary tribute to Jefferies. Although a naturalist, Hudson described in some detail the often squalid conditions of the Sussex towns and their inhabitants one hundred years ago.

Richard Jefferies' (1848-1887) short life was marred by mental and physical illness, and it was during the last four years of his life that he lived in Sussex, first at Crowborough, then Hove, and finally Goring. Jefferies is rightly remembered as a writer of the countryside; yet his observant and often amusing descriptions of life in Brighton and Hove in the 1880s should not be overlooked. Although Jefferies never lived to write a 'Sussex' book, it is clear from surviving notes and essays that he had such a project in mind.

E.V. Lucas (1866-1937) was one of the most respected journalists of his day. He had begun his working life as an apprentice in Treacher's bookshop in Brighton. Lucas was one of the early travel writers and transversed the globe, writing features for magazines and newspapers. His 'Highways and Byways in

Sussex', published in 1904, is a gem of a book, being both popular yet also learned. The book is greatly enhanced by Frederick Griggs' superb line drawings, some of which are reproduced in this book.

You will also find references to Michael Fairless and Rudyard Kipling, (see under Henfield and Burwash respectively). Failure on my part to mention other 'great' Sussex writers, such as S.P.B. Mais or Barclay Wills is due partly to limited space and also to my lack of knowledge of these authors' writings.

A Place-name Index and a Literary Index are found at the end of the book.

Final word

I hope you will enjoy reading this book and that it will encourage you to delve deeper into the history of the county. One of the best ways of keeping in touch with the latest research in Sussex history is by joining the Sussex Archaeological Society, which publishes an annual journal and a newsletter every four months. For details telephone the society on (01273) 405737.

Chris Hare
Worthing
3 September 1998

Shoeing an Ox at Saddlescombe

The author is indebted to the following people, who paid for a copy of this book in advance, and then waited patiently for between six and eighteen months for their copy to arrive. Thank you all very much!

S. Abrahams, Horsham

M. I. Atkin-Berry, Arundel

W. Barker, Worthing

Peter Barnes, Haywards Heath

C. J. Barnett, Horsham

Richard Beeny, Chichester

Sqdrn. Ldr. Dennis Bird, Shoreham

Doreen Bishop, Corbridge (Northumberland)

Enid and David Brindley, Rustington

R. A. Brown, Newhaven

Niela Bull, Worthing

A. Burns, Pagham

Wendy Capon, Rustington

Peter Cittenden, Seaford

Ernest Clark, Steyning

Mary Clifton Everest, Worthing

Mrs Coats, Worthing

E. T. Coles, Littlehampton

Jenny Coles, Bognor Regis

John Cotter, Burgess Hill

G. Coxon, Worthing

B. V. Davies, Storrington

Madge Dickins, Chichester

S. M. Duggan, Shoreham

Una Durk, Worthing

S. Ellis, Newhaven

E. Evans, Lancing

Kathleen Fancourt, Chichester

K. F. M. Farrance, Rogate

G. Frankenhoff, Rottingdean

Jim French, Billingshurst

P. C. Finch, Lancing

Mike Gammon, Arundel

Jean Godden, Worthing

D. M. Gold, Burpham

Elizabeth Greaves, Bognor Regis

Stanley J. Grible, Haywards Heath

K. M. Hadfield, Emsworth

Kathryn Haigh, Pulborough

Joyce Hall, Shoreham

Marjorie Hallam, Graffham

M. Hamblin, Lancing

K. B. Hampton, Chichester

Simon Hollingworth, Storrington

Jean Holmes-Clark, Chichester

P. M. Hewitt, Newhaven

D. Howey, Sompting

J Instance, Emsworth

David Jarman JP, East Preston

Malcolm Kenworthy, Bognor Regis

S. Kidd, Bognor Regis

John S. Kitchen, Arundel

Athalie Knowles, Goring

B. V. Langford, Worthing

Fred Lilley, East Wittering

D. Lloyd-Bottom, Goring

P. J. Long, Goring

Mercia MacDermott, Worthing

Roger Mann, Littlehampton

Gwyn E. Mansfield, Haywards Heath

R. Marchant, Southwick

E. P. Marsden, Southwick
J. M. Maskell, Worthing
M. McCarthy, Goring
G. and N. Miles, Horsham
R. N. More, Shoreham
Frank Morley, Brighton
Joan Mullins, Worthing
John Munro, Arundel
D. Newton, Worthing
Mrs. Nield, Worthing
Jim Noble, Nutbourne
D. A. Norton, Ashington
R. B. Owens, Chichester
John Parker, Arundel
C. A. Pearson, Worthing
Bess Plested, Emsworth
M. A. Puttock, Haywards Heath
Bill Price, Ford
Ann Rattray, Horsham
M. H. Reed, Chichester
C. D. & R.A. Reynolds, Billingshurst
Tony Reynolds, Angmering
M. A. Richards, West Wittering
D. Riddle, Bognor Regis
Mary Ridley, Seaford
Adge Roberts, East Preston
Glad Roberts, Lancing
Peter Robinson, Chichester
Eileen Rodgers, Brighton
J. Roseveare, Rodmell
Angela Rushton, Goring
M. Searle, Horsham,
Mary D. Secretan, East Preston
Betty Sheppard, Oving

D. Simmons, Seaford
G. J. and K. L. Slay, Chichester
Sir Harold Smedley, Ferring
Edna Smith, Bognor Regis
Cicely Snead, Lancing
Cynthia Soleiri, Chichester
Gerald and Pat Spain, Horsham
J. Spofforth, Slindon
M. J. Steptoe, Horsham
Peter & Judy Stern, Bosham
A. Stevens, Worthing
E. Stonefield, Worthing
J. Stoton, Barnham
Molly Sutcliffe, Barnham
Micheal Tanner, Ferring
T. M. Tanner, Findon Valley,
Worthing
Edwina Targett, Billingshurst
Dudley and Rosemary Tee,
Rottingdean
Mr. & Mrs. I. C. Thompson,
Haywards Heath
Alec Tritton, Barnham
Barry and Elizabeth Venn, East
Grinstead
Micheal Verrall, Dorking
Roberta Vickery, Horsham
D. Watt, Worthing
Vaughan Willshaw, Rottingdean
Mary and John Winton, Balcombe

CHICHESTER & THE WESTERN DOWNS

Chichester is the cathedral city of Sussex, and arguably its oldest settlement, having been founded by the British tribe known as the Regni, some two thousand years ago. This tribe had the good sense to co-operate with, rather than resist the Roman invasion of 43AD. As a result the Regni were handsomely rewarded, and their chieftains were granted Roman citizenship. Agricultural produce from the rich coastal plain of western Sussex was exported across the Roman Empire. These Romano-British farmers became very wealthy, and lived in splendid villas, attended by armies of servants. The largest of these villas, a palace in fact, was built at Fishbourne, and may have been the home of the Regni king, Togidubnus. Fishbourne Palace is owned by the Sussex Archaeological Society, and is open to the public.

Chichester Cathedral 1938 (WSCC)

Chichester's well preserved city walls date back to Roman times, although they were rebuilt and re-fortified on several occasions. The Saxons built a fortress here to defend themselves against Viking raiders (see p25). During the troubled reign of King John, in 1215, the French stormed the city, and held it for over a year. After John's death, the city was recaptured, and the wooden fortress in the north-east of the city was demolished (the mound on which it stood can still be seen in Priory Park). During the English Civil War, in December 1642, the city was besieged by Parliamentary forces, and ultimately forced to surrender (see p78).

Chichester Cathedral was built by the Normans, and was as much a symbol of their political power as it was of their religious piety. The stone for its construction was actually shipped over from Normandy; little wonder then that it took over one hundred years to complete! The original Saxon cathedral at Selsey was abandoned, and was eventually swept away by coastal erosion. Chichester Cathedral has not been lucky, it has twice been damaged by fire, was once hit by a thunderbolt, has been shaken by earth tremors, and most recently, in 1861, its spire collapsed. Throughout the 1980's and 90's, extensive restoration work has been undertaken on the cathedral, resulting in a suspiciously 'new' look to parts of the current stonework.

Visitors to the cathedral soon notice the detached bell-tower, which appears to be very eroded in comparison to the main body of the cathedral. Despite its appearance, the tower is actually of more recent construction than the cathedral, but is built of Isle of Wight sandstone, a rock that weathers more readily than the Caen limestone used in the construction of the cathedral proper. The bell tower was built because it was thought, with good reason, that the tower of the cathedral, weakened by fire and the rest, would not be able to sustain the weight of the great cast-iron bells.

Over the years, Chichester has had some flamboyant and controversial Bishops, from Wifrid himself, who converted the South Saxons to Christianity (see p22), to Bishop Bell, whose comments on unemployment and the dropping of the Atomic bombs on Japan, proved contentious in more recent history. Perhaps it is Bishop Richard (later Saint Richard), who served during the reign of Henry III, who is best remembered. Unlike his immediate predecessor, Ralph Neville, who lived

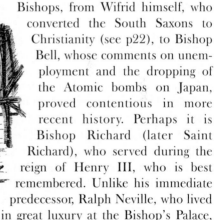

The old kitchens at the Bishops Palace (WSCC)

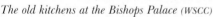

in great luxury at the Bishop's Palace, and became Lord Chancellor of England, Richard wore a humble cassock, with a hair shirt underneath, and dined exclusively on vegetables, the diet of a peasant. As Bishop he rooted out corruption and superstitious practice in the diocese, including the random opening of the Bible for the purpose of divination. He was truly loved by the poor of Sussex, to whom he channelled much of his charitable efforts. He died shortly after preaching a sermon in favour of the crusades. Within ten years he had been canonised, and his shrine became a focus for pilgrims throughout the medieval period.

The interior of the cathedral contains much of interest, and volunteer guides escort parties of visitors on a regular basis. Of particular interest is the fragment of Roman mosaic, a survival from the Roman Basilica, which stood on the site of the cathedral. Most impressive are the twelfth century stone panels in the south aisle, depicting various scenes from the gospels. They were removed either during the Reformation or civil war and only re-discovered by workmen, restoring the choir stalls in 1829.

The city of Chichester today is a by-word for respectability and affluence. The ring-road created around the city some thirty years ago, allowed the enlightened planners of the time to pedestrianise Chichester's four ancient streets (South Street, West Street, North Street and East Street). Had this not been done, in the teeth of much local opposition, the traffic congestion, bad enough in the late 'sixties, would be truly horrific today. So the apparently timeless air of tranquillity is of recent creation. Indeed it is only just outside of living memory when Chichester was described in the most unflattering of terms, by the naturalist and writer, W.H. Hudson. Writing in 1899, Hudson claimed there was nothing quiet or beautiful about Chichester, nor indeed holy. He complained that the city was smelly and depressing, but worst of all, he said were the inhabitants themselves, many of whom were noisy and drunk -

"In the streets, near the railway station, at the Market Cross, and at various corners, you will see groups of the most utterly drink-degraded wretches it is possible to find anywhere in the kingdom - men with soulless faces and watery eyes, dressed like tramps - standing idle with their hands in their pockets. But there is not a penny there, or they would not be standing in the mud and rain; and as for doing any work, they are past that. Here that rare spectacle, a man without a shirt, has met my sight, not once or twice, but several times, the naked flesh showing through the rents of a ragged jacket buttoned or pinned up to the neck. These loathly human objects are strangely incongruous at the spot, under the great spire, in sight of the green open healthy downs, in perhaps the richest agricultural district in England."

The Chichester authorities were stung by the ferocity of Hudson's attack, and a few years later they responded by revoking the licences of nearly half of the city's drinking establishments. Writing in 1903, E.V.Lucas tried to balance Hudson's 'caustic chapter', and declared that Chichester was "always a cathedral town," and that, "whatever noise may be in the air you know in your heart that quietude is its true characteristic."

Chichester has certainly seen peaks and troughs in its long history. One trough followed the ravages of the civil war, and lasted some fifty years. The turnaround can be dated from the building of Westgate House in 1696. This fine Jacobean building, which stands in West Street, was the home of John Edes, after whom it is now named. In the early 1990's, the county council, who own **Edes' House**, spent one and a half million pounds on its restoration (the building having been neglected for many years). West Sussex residents may like to approach their local county councillor to arrange a tour of the building; after all, they helped pay for its conservation!

In 1712, in the poor and run-down, south-east quadrant of Chichester, known as the Pallants, Henry Peckham, a millionaire wine-importer (notice how the wealth of the city was built on alcohol- related trades!), built an imposing, brick-built mansion. **Pallant House**, as it became known, must have seemed strange indeed, surrounded by miserable tenements, but within a generation the district was transformed out of all recognition. Fashionable brick and stuccoed terraces emerged from the squalor, and in the place of the former residents came the professional classes, who, it will be observed still work from premises in the Pallants to the present day.

In North Street, the Butter Market and the Council House (or City Hall) were built shortly after the Pallant development, and symbolised the city's new prosperity. Early in the following century the Corn Exchange, a giant of a building with cast-iron columns holding up a Greek-style portico, was erected in East Street. Earlier this century it was converted into cinema, and more recently the front portion was converted into an outlet for the burger-chain, MacDonalds.

At the eastern end of East Street are found St. Pancras, and the Hornet. It was here that the poorer classes lived, just outside of the city walls. The St. Pancraens were traditionally fierce Protestants, and keen Orangemen. The Corporation of St. Pancras, a Protestant society established in order to commemorate the ascension to the throne of William of Orange in 1689, still exists, but its objects are now purely social and charitable.

Other buildings well worth a visit include St. Mary's, a medieval chapel and almshouse in St. Martins; the former guildhall and greyfriars chapel in Priory Park, and the Market Cross, commissioned five centuries ago by Bishop Storey, and rightly regarded as one of the most impressive of its type anywhere in the country.

The Market Cross C.1860 (WSCC)

Within easy reach of Chichester is **Bognor Regis**. This somewhat despoiled seaside town was designed to be a resort for Royalty. It was the brainchild of Sir Richard Hotham, millionaire businessman and former Member of Parliament. Inspired by the development of Brighton, Hotham hoped to create a resort of the very highest calibre, all to be financed from his own personal fortune. By the time he died in 1799, the project was only partially completed. His own home, Hotham House was there, as were the lavish villas to the north, such as the Dome House, but his hopes of 'Hothampton' living on after his death were dashed. With the exception of Waterloo Square, a pleasing Regency development on the seafront, little of architectural note was built in Bognor after Sir

Richard's death. The suffix 'Regis' was added in 1929, following the convalescence in the town of King George V.

Pagham harbour is located on the western side of Bognor. The area is a nature reserve, and a haven for all types of wildlife, especially wildfowl. During the Victorian period, 'sportsmen' came from all over the country, in order to shoot the various wild birds that congregated here, a practise that was only banned by the county council in recent years. At the entrance to the harbour there was once an aquatic phenomena known as the 'Hushing Pool', which appeared at certain tides, causing the sea to bubble and froth, as if it were boiling. During the nineteenth century the harbour was drained, and the land reclaimed for agriculture. The sea broke through again after the Great Storm of 1913, but although the 'harbour' was reinstated, the Hushing Pool was not, and so just remains as a curious historical footnote. The church of St. Thomas a Becket at Pagham retains some original Norman features.

Selsey is famous today as being a victim of the weather: flooding and tornadoes have been regular occurrences. In Saxon times it was separated from the mainland and known as Seal Island. It was from here that St. Wilfrid (see p22) is supposed to have begun his mission to convert the South Saxons to Christianity. By the time of Alfred, the South Saxon See was centred on Selsey, and a cathedral (small by later standards) had been built here. Coastal erosion washed away the cathedral, and is still eating away at Selsey to this day. It was not until 1809 that a raised causeway was constructed to take a road over the marshland to Selsey, before then you had to take the ferry, or chance your luck in wading over the marshes. From 1897 to 1935 a light railway, known as the Selsey Tramway operated from Chichester. The little town was also once famous for being the home of Colin Pullinger, who patented a 'Humane Mousetrap' in 1857. His factory was producing hundreds of the contraptions by the 1880's.

Bosham is another place long-associated with the Saxon past. It was said that King Canute (see p26) tried to turn back the waves here. Legend long insisted that Canute's daughter was buried at Bosham, and sure enough in Victorian times, the remains of a young girl, later dated to the time of Canute, were discovered under the stone floor of the church, buried in a fine coffin. Bosham church has many Saxon features, including its tower. Legend relates how a raiding party of Vikings stole the bells from Bosham church, but as the raiders made their escape, the bells broke through the bottom of their vessel, and so bells and raiders were lost forever to the sea. The famous Bayeux Tapestry features Bosham church, and shows the local lord, Harold Godwinson, soon to be King of England, at prayer (see p27).

To the north of Chichester is the hamlet of West Stoke, from where one may walk to **Kingly Vale**, famous for its ancient yew trees (see p25). The Downs north of Chichester are some of the most unspoilt in Sussex. On the Trundle can be found an Iron Age 'hillfort', which was built over earlier prehistoric remains. To the north of Kingly Vale, just off the B2141, is the Royal Oak at Hooksway. This pub, until the early 1970's was run by a very elderly couple, who made no concessions to the twentieth century in terms of facilities; the beer was home-brewed, the floor was spit and sawdust, and the toilet arrangements consisted in a chamber pot for the women, and the outside field for the men. Visitors should be reassured (or disappointed?) to learn that considerable improvements have taken place in the intervening years. From the Royal Oak it is possible to walk up to the 'Devil's Jumps', six Bronze Age barrows, which are maintained by the Society of Sussex Downsmen.

To the west of Chichester is **Boxgrove**, an unremarkable village, with a very remarkable church. The church is all that now survives of Boxgrove Priory, once one of the largest religious houses in Sussex (see p50). It was in a disused gravel quarry in the adjacent parish of Halnaker, that archaeologists discovered 'Boxgrove Man', the oldest identified hominid ever unearthed in the British Isles. The excava-

The Devils Jumps

tions began in 1982 and continued until 1996. Although the discovery of the 500,000 year old tibia proved the most newsworthy event of the excavations, other equally important, if less sensational finds were also located. Those wishing to be acquainted with the full story are advised to read Dr. Mark Roberts book, *Fairweather Eden*, which details the whole sixteen year excavation.

If in the Chichester area, visitors are advised to visit **Barnham**, not so much to view the remnants of the old Arun to Portsmouth Canal, or to appreciate the Jacobean dignity of Barnham Court, but to visit the Murrell Arms. Run for the last thirty-four years by Mervyn and Daphne Cutten, the Murrell Arms remains true to the old ethos of a country pub. No jukebox here, or fancy food, just good beer, and straightforward ploughman's lunches (no garnish accompaniments, or the inflated prices that go with them). The Murrell Arms is a museum of pub memorabilia, and local history, and is quite unique.

Road-rolling at Barham C.1920 (WSCC)

MIDHURST & PETWORTH

Midhurst and Petworth are both ancient market towns, whose very existence has been dominated by powerful, resident landowners. At Petworth, the Earls of Northumberland, and later the Earls of Egremont kept a tight control over life in the town for many centuries from the opulence of Petworth House. Midhurst was similarly served by the Viscounts Montague, who lived and ruled at Cowdray House until 1793. There was a rivalry between the two places, and between the two landowners, which actually took the form of armed conflict during the English Civil War, when Northumberland sided with Parliament, while Montague upheld the King's cause (see pages 74 to 86).

Although close to Hampshire, these are very much Sussex towns, as Ian Nairn appreciated when he visited in 1965, as part of his collaboration with Nikolaus Pevsner on their mammoth survey of English architecture -

"To the main-road traveller, Midhurst, like Petworth, is a bewildering series of acute ninety-degree bends combined with an inexplicable cottagey cosiness in the buildings, so different from the open market-places of Hampshire. Few towns are more deceptive, few towns withhold themselves so firmly until the traveller gets out of his car and onto his feet: few towns have a more exciting relationship with the surrounding countryside. Almost all of this must be due to the careful eye kept on the town by the owners of Cowdray."

Cowdray House is today a ruin, and has been since fire gutted it in 1793.

Cowdray House ruins in 1903 (FG)

It was originally built in the late fifteenth and early sixteenth centuries, by four successive owners. It was Sir William Fitzwilliam, later created Earl of Southampton, who added the distinctive gatehouse and hexagonal towers in the 1530's. After his death, Cowdray passed to Sir Anthony Browne, later created Viscount Montague, who gained more than any other man from the dissolution of the monasteries in Sussex (see p51) In 1591, Queen Elizabeth visited Cowdray. Montague and his sons had been the first aristocratic family in the country to put themselves at their sovereign's disposal when news of the approaching Spanish Armada first reached these shores in 1588. Queen Elizabeth was keen to repay such loyalty. After being received with full pomp and ceremony on the Saturday evening, the following days were given over to merriment. Basing his account on a contemporary source, Lucas described the scene -

"These preliminaries over, the fun began. At breakfast next morning three oxen and a hundred and forty geese were devoured. On Monday, August 17th, Elizabeth rode to her bower in the park, took a crossbow from a nymph who sang a sweet song, and with it shot 'three or four' deer, carefully brought within range. After dinner, standing on one of the turrets she watched sixteen bucks 'pulled down with greyhounds' in the lawn. On Tuesday, the Queen was approached by a pilgrim, who first called her 'Fairest of all creatures,' and expressed the wish that the world might end with her life and then led her to an oak whereon were hanging escutcheons of her Majesty and all the neighbouring noblemen and gentlemen. As she looked, a 'wild man' clad in ivy appeared and delivered an address on the importance of loyalty. On Wednesday, the Queen was taken to a goodlie fish pond where was an angler. After some words from him a band of fishermen approached, drawing their nets after them, whereupon the angler, turning to her Majesty, remarked that her virtue made envy blush and stand amazed. Having thus spoken, the net was drawn and found to be full of fish, which were laid at Elizabeth's feet ...On Thursday the lords and ladies dined at a table forty-eight yards long, and there was a country dance with tabor and pipe, which drew from her Majesty 'gentle applause.' On Friday, the Queen knighted six gentlemen and passed on to Chichester."

The very essence of 'Merrie England' is conjured up by such a description. It was certainly a great week for the aristocracy and gentry of the district. The peasantry of course were not invited to such events, but the prosperity and success of their lord, would at least guarantee some stability and security in their own lives.

There are several buildings in **Midhurst** which date back to Elizabethan times, and not benefiting from the 'sophistication' of eighteenth century Chichester or Lewes. Many of them were spared the re-fronting in the classical style, which took place wholesale in the two county towns. The Old Market House is an obvious example. The only major alteration here is that the ground floor was originally open. The Spread Eagle, with its timber-framed over-hang is an archetypal English inn, one on which so many 'mock-Tudor' public houses of the 1930's took their cue. The Swan is also believed to date back to about 1600. Then there is the evocatively named Knockhundred Row, part of which contains the county library.

Hudson has plenty to say about Midhurst, and for the most part his comments are complimentary compared to his observations regarding Chichester -

"... I went to Midhurst, on the other side of the downs, to find myself in a small, old, and extremely picturesque town, which, in its rough-paved, crooked, uneven streets, ancient timbered houses, its curfew bell, and darkness and silence at night, seemed to have suddenly carried me back into mediaeval times. But in spite of its hoary aspect and air of antiquity and remoteness and the number of inns, some very large, clustering around the central part, I felt as I wandered aimlessly about, and talked, when a chance offered, to workingmen and with cottage women and children, that I had come into a different and better moral atmosphere."

Hudson's efforts to gain a lodging for the night did not prove too successful. In most of the inns he noticed only 'a faint glimmer' at the windows. At one inn, probably the Spread Eagle, he found all the doors locked, but eventually after groping down a 'dim passage', he managed to rouse a woman, who let him inside. The whole place was dark, and there were no fires. The woman explained that they had not been expecting any visitors, so had made no provision. Eventually Hudson was led into the landlord's private quarters, which he described in none too flattering terms, there being dirt and rubbish everywhere. The landlord himself was seated at a plain table, eating a meal which consisted of bread, cheese and onions. The two men talked for over an hour, chiefly on the decline of the inn business in Midhurst, and the lengths to which the landlords had to go to in order to make a living -

"I learnt that formerly there were more public-houses in the town, but some had been compelled to close, and that others were given by the owners, the brewers, rent free. My host paid not one penny rent for the grand old house he occupied, and even so he could hardly make a decent living out of it. Certainly his evening meal had not struck me as too luxurious and expensive. Another tenant of an ancient house close by was in even a worse case. The landlord, to make ends meet and save the house, had conceived the happy idea of providing sleeping accommodation to poor vagrants at fourpence a night. He had gone into the byways and hedges for his guests, and his house had become well known to all the tramps and beggars that infest that part of Sussex."

These same inns today are most exclusive, and a bed for the night would cost rather more than fourpence! In case we should suspect Hudson of exaggeration, corroboration comes from another source. Writing a decade later, Tickner Edwardes, passed close by on his tramp from Torquay to Burpham. The rain was coming down in torrents, and in order to try and keep dry, he had 'borrowed' the clothes off a scarecrow, to put over the top of his own. On reaching **Elstead**, he presented a pitiful spectacle, but none-the-less received a welcome from the local road-mender, the first such welcome he had received all day -

" He was a serene old man with bow-legs and mild blue eyes; and he seemed to have the village to himself, save that, from the little schoolhouse hard by, there came the low tumult of children's voices. I stopped really to listen to this pleasant rivulet of sound stemming out upon the dismal twilight. But the old man mistook the action. He gave over scraping in the gutter, and looked cheerfully my way.

'Travellin' be ye?' said he with a pleasant nod.

In his voice there was a kind, hearty ring that strangely

Tickner Edwardes
(WSCC)

affected me. It was the first genial word and look I had received for many a long hour. I drew a little nearer.

'Yes; I've come a long way, and it's hard going in the rain. Have you seen many of my sort passing through today?'

He thought a little, his chin on the handle of his hoe.

'Noa!' said he at length. 'Plenty o' other sorts, but nane o' your sort.'

'What sort do you take me to be, then?'

He hesitated, and I could see he was casting about for a gentle way to put it.

'Ah!' he said presently, chopping away at the weeds again. 'Trouble comes, an' comes to high an' low. I ha' seed it, an' I knows. Jedge not, an' ye wun't be jedged - that's what I allers says.'

This somehow nettled me. I was willing to pass as an out-and-out, incorrigible tramp, but to be taken for a broken down gentleman had in it a mysterious quality of offence. I wondered whether it would have hurt me at all, or hurt me more, if my case had been as he suspected.

'Where does that road lead to?' I asked him.

He shook the water from his hat.

'That there? 'A goes by Stedham on to Mid-'ust. 'Twill be your road, I reckon.'

'Why my road?'

I could see he was in difficulty again.

'Well, now, they others - they mostly arsts fer that way.'

'For Midhurst?'

'Aye!' He stopped, and then surprised me by flushing red to his hat-brim. 'Mid'ust, ye know. The-th' labourin'-'ouse. No offence, mister, I do hope; that I do!'

We were both in the same confusion now.

'No,' I said; 'I'm not thinking of going there tonight. I hate towns. Where does that other road take you to?'

'That'n? Through Bepton to Cocking. Purty nigh fower mile 'tis. But ye're a smartish bit wet a'ready, mister, beant't yer?'

I told him I was dry enough underneath. Whereupon, by no means misunderstanding me, he nevertheless went to his basket that was tucked under the ivy of the school wall and drew forth a tin bottle.

''Tis home-brewed,' he said. 'An y'are very welcome. Water ye've had to-day, an' to spare; so a change o' liquor wun't harm ye.'

I drank gratefully to the fine, sensitive-souled old man, devoutly hoping that there were more like him in the land."

Petworth House dates from 1309, when permission was granted to crenellate the existing manor house. In Elizabeth's time the house was enlarged, and then totally rebuilt in 1682. The Duke of Somerset married the Earl of

Northumberland's eldest daughter, and since the Earl had no surviving sons, the estate passed to Somerset. It was he who created the present house, which is built in the French style. Later the hunting grounds around the house was laid out in a formal fashion by the famous landscape gardener, Capability Brown. About a century later, George O'Brien Wyndham, 3rd Earl of Egremont became the patron of many of the great artists of his day, including Turner, many of whose great works are still on display in the house. Egremont was heavily involved in local politics. Towards the end of his long life, in the 1830's, he arranged several sailings of emigrant ships from West Sussex, taking the poor of the county to a new life in Canada.

"Petworth", declared Nairn in 1965, "must have a by-pass". The old-world market town, with its narrow streets was not designed for modern motor traffic. Thirty-three years later Petworth is still waiting, and will continue to wait, for the problem is insoluble. For once, it is not only cost which is a factor, it is also a question of where to put the by-pass, either through Petworth Park to the west, or the Shimmings valley to the east. About twenty years ago there were proposals for a route through the Park, but the National Trust, who own both Park and House objected. They pointed out that the proposed route would go straight through the wild deer's rutting ground: far better to build the by-pass through the Shimmings valley. "Not on your life", said the people of Petworth, "thats our rutting ground!" And so the matter has rested ever since. There was talk of constructing a tunnel under the Park, but it would be very expensive, and the portals could prove unsightly. It does seem incredible that neither national nor European funding can be made available to finance such a project, but apparently all avenues have been explored. At the time of writing (1998), there is a ban on heavy traffic in Petworth, which now has to follow alternative routes.

Petworth Almshouses 1903 (FG)

Traffic aside, Petworth is a remarkable place, its history seems to cling to every brick and tile. It is also very well-to-do. House prices are high, and would be higher still if it were not for the traffic. Petworth is the only place in Sussex that I know of where you'll find a pub with an entry phone. Yet sometimes too much wealth can be as damaging for a place as too much poverty. Even some the shops in Petworth look as if they have been transported from the corner of an exclusive West-end store.

The Market Place is dominated by the Town Hall, and its eye-catching bust of William III. (this is a copy, the original is in Petworth House). 'King Billy's' presence is a reminder of the strongly held Protestant beliefs that survived here until quite recent times. Opposite the Town Hall is a fine Georgian building, covered in wisteria. A close examination of its windows reveals several of them to be fakes, craftily painted onto the stonework. Presumably the original windows were blocked up at the time of William Pitt's window tax, and never subsequently reinstated.

The Window Tax was introduced as a substitute for the excessive duty then applied to tea, which had led to an epidemic of smuggling (see p118) Pitt hoped that the new tax arrangements would be both unavoidable, and would also lead to a decline in smuggling. He was wrong on both counts. Smugglers often referred to themselves as 'free traders', a cause made respectable in the 1850's, when a policy of Free Trade was adopted by the new Liberal government. No man did more to bring about this reversal in economic thinking than Richard Cobden of West Lavington. Cobden had been born on his father's farm at Heyshott, and grew up in an era when smuggling gangs prowled the countryside. The economic crisis of the 1820's forced the family to sell the farm, and young Richard became a commercial traveller. Cobden realised that restriction on trade not only harmed the economy, it also created a whole criminal class that would not otherwise exist. He became a prominent figure in the new Liberal Party, and was elected to Parliament, becoming a key figure in the Liberal governments of the 1850's and 60's. Cobden's thesis proved correct, and by his death, in 1865, the armed gangs of his boyhood had disappeared, and the British economy had become the strongest in the world. He had also been able to buy back his father's old farm, only a short distance from Dunford House, his Sussex home.

The little River Rother flows close to Midhurst and Petworth, nestling peacefully between them and the Downs. It was while ambling along this route that Hudson met a man who told him with absolute certainty that this countryside was the very best that could be found. Hudson, who was a great traveller, of course would have none of this, telling the man it was simply a delusion based on sentiment for the place of one's birth. Later, however, he regretted his tone, and wrote -

W H Hudson (WSCC)

"I fancy that after all I did not convince him of his error. I rather hope not. For now when I recall the scenes we looked upon together - that wild stream of the Rother; the small old-world peaceful villages; the hills of so pure and fresh a green, their lower slopes and valleys purple and dark with beech and pine; when I find how persistently it all comes back to me, and how vivid and beautiful the impression is, I am not quite sure that I was wholly right in my philosophy, and that his delusion was nothing but a delusion."

THE SAXON & NORMAN HERITAGE

Sussex was founded by settlers from what is now Germany and the Netherlands, about 1,500 years ago. These people created their own kingdom, the land of the South Saxons, from which we get the modern name of Sussex. On this point at least there is general agreement, however probe a little deeper, ask a few more questions, about how and why Sussex came into existence, and diverging views soon emerge.

For a long time the creation of Sussex was explained in terms of violent invasion and bloody slaughter. No longer able to defend their British territories, the Romans left the people here to the mercy of invading Saxons, Angles, and Jutes. Many, perhaps most were put to the sword, while the survivors fled westwards, to Wales, and to Cornwall.

More recently, some historians have put a different gloss on events, depicting the incoming peoples, not as invaders, but as a fifth century version of economic migrants. Instead of blood and guts, we are presented with a far more mundane picture of gradual assimilation between Britons and Saxons.

The Anglo-Saxon Chronicle (ASC) gives a dramatic personalised picture of events during the fifth century. It describes how Vortigern, the 'proud tyrant' of the native Britons living in south-east England, tried to secure his kingdom by inviting in mercenaries to help protect it. Led by Hengest and Horsa, these warriors defeated all Vortigern's enemies, in return they were granted land. Soon however they wanted more land, and turned against Vortigern and his people, "destroying through fire and the sword's edge."

Eventually the whole of what is now Kent was lost, and still the fighting continued. Confusingly the ASC talks about the 'Welsh': "The Welsh fled the English as one flees fire." By Welsh, the chroniclers meant the Britons. Eventually, the Britons were confined to what is now modern Wales, and Cornwall (once known as West Wales). It is worth realising that English and British, were not one and the same, indeed at this stage in history they were two very different and apparently warring peoples.

From a Sussex point of view, a crucial entry in the ASC comes in 477 -

Old Shoreham Church in 1850 (WSCC)

"Aella came to Britain, and his three sons Cymen, Wlencing and Cyssa, with three ships, landing at the place called Cymensora. There they killed many Welsh, and drove some in flight into the Weald." Aella was a Saxon, those who had taken Kent were Jutes. Where 'Cymensora' actually was is not known, for a long time it was believed to be at Selsey, but it could have been further east, possibly at Shoreham.

In the year 485, the chroniclers tell us that, "Aella fought the Welsh on the bank near Merecredesburna." Again the site of this battle is not known, although it might well have been by a river. The Saxons had broken an earlier treaty with the Britons, and crossed the 'Merecredesburna', the boundary that had been agreed between the two. The Saxons now wanted all the Britons' lands. The war continued for another six years, until it was concluded with the final rout of the Britons at Pevensey in 491 -

"Aella and Cyssa besieged Anderida [the Roman-built fort], near Pevensey, and killed all who were inside, so there was not one Briton left."

These early entries in the Anglo-Saxon Chronicle formed part of the oral tradition of the English, and it was several hundreds of years before they were written down, which has caused some modern scholars to cast doubt on their reliability, dismissing these blood-curdling accounts as little more than fables. However other accounts, written down at the time or shortly afterwards, by the likes of Nennius, or the priest Gildas, largely confirm the account in the ASC. To this can be added the work of the Venerable Bede, who was also writing some centuries later. Bede tells us that Aella, the first king of the South Saxons, was also 'Bretwalda' or overlord of all the English living south of the Humber.

Such evidence might appear conclusive, were it not for the archaeological record, which tells a rather different story. Had these written accounts being wholly correct, then one would expect evidence of slaughter, and evidence presumably of burnt and razed towns and villages. Curiously such evidence does exist for the earlier centuries, when England was still under Roman rule. Fire did destroy Romano-British habitations in Sussex during the third and fourth centuries. Examples of this nature can be found in minor sites, such as the temple at Lancing Ring, or prominent sites, such as the palace at Fishbourne.

There can be little doubt that raids by pirates did occur, there was destruction, and almost certainly loss of life. But does that account for the end of the Romano-British culture in Sussex, or are there other clues to consider? The archaeology suggests there are. Excavations have revealed Saxon settlements existing in coastal Sussex at the same time as Romano-British ones. Two main sites have emerged: between the rivers Ouse and Cuckmere, and at Highdown, north of Ferring and Goring.

The Highdown site, which consists of over one hundred Saxon pagan burials, dates to the first half of the fifth century, a time when the Romano-British farmstead or 'villa' was still operating, only a mile away at Northbrook. Such a situation hardly seems compatible with the idea of terrible, merciless warfare. It has been suggested that the warriors buried on the hill were actually mercenaries, hired by the farmers at Northbrook to defend them against marauders, but that is only conjecture.

It is perhaps worth considering conditions in the homeland of the Saxons during the fifth century (I use the term 'Saxons' loosely, for there were several different ethnic groups involved in the English settlement). The archaeology from the Netherlands, northern Germany and Denmark for this period reveals a crisis, brought about by human activity and climatic conditions. Large numbers of peoples were fleeing from the fighting in central Europe occasioned by the assaults being made on the Roman Empire's eastern borders by the Goths, Vandals and Huns. These refugees fled into the lands of the Jutes, Angles and Saxons. It could not have been at a worse time, for rising sea levels brought about by warmer conditions, were causing large areas of agricultural land to be lost to the sea.

People living by the coast tried to save themselves by building large mounds as places of refuge, known as 'terpen', but in the long term the situation was clearly not sustainable. Many looked for new land, better land, land with fewer inhabitants. Not far away, across the sea, were the rich fertile plains of Sussex, plains which may well have been largely uninhabited at this point in history. The evidence suggests that most of the large Romano-British farms in Sussex had been abandoned fifty, even a hundred years before the Saxon settlement took place.

Chichester, the capital of the Regni, and one of the most important cities in south-east England, began a slow and irreversible decline in about 350AD, over a century before the events described in the Anglo-Saxon Chronicle. It must be remembered that the wealth and success of Chichester was based on trade. Regni merchants traded right across the Roman Empire, it was the 'free market' of its day. Once that trade was disrupted by war, and once the Romans were no longer able to offer military protection to merchant vessels, the trade gradually withered away, and with it the good life of villas, bath houses, and the armies of servants needed to sustain such opulence.

By the time the Saxon began to settle permanently in Sussex it is to be wondered just how many 'Britons' were living here at all. The wealthier ones may have travelled to safer parts of the Empire, taking what was left of their wealth with them. As for the ordinary folk, some may have migrated to the west, where for a time at least there was some stability. Others remained; how many we may never know. Some may well have perished by the sword, or even from want of food and raiment. Yet others must have survived and been assimilated with the incomers. Were this not so, the genetic make-up of the English would not be as varied and unique as it is and our resemblance to the present day inhabitants of Germany and the Nordic countries would surely be more striking.

There is however one more important piece of evidence to consider: place names. It has been said that no county in the whole of England has such an overwhelming preponderance of place names with Saxon origins as Sussex. One noted Saxon scholar, Martin Welch, could find only a handful of place names in Sussex which could be demonstrated to have elements derived from a Latin, that is to say, Romano-British origin. The Latin word 'campus', meaning open space, is recognisable in Warningcamp (a hamlet near Arundel), although the first part of the word almost certainly refers to a Saxon chief or tribe. Another common Latin word, 'portus', meaning port or harbour, can be recognised in the modern-day place-name of Portslade.

Considering the success of Roman Sussex, particularly in the western part of the county, coupled with the large population that existed here, the dearth of place names from that period appears ominous. However if, as seems likely, civic society had broken down some time before the Saxons came, and large areas of the county were abandoned and depopulated, then it is hardly surprising that so few of the old names survive. Much, though that was older did survive. The borders of the territory in which the Regni lived are not known exactly, though at one time they may have extended from Portchester in the west, to Pevensey in the east. A closer look at the distribution of key Roman sites - of villas, potteries, tile workings and temples, finds the majority of them existing within the borders of modern-day West Sussex. Certainly the boundary between the old South Saxon kingdom, and its larger neighbour, Wessex, has changed little over the centuries. Close to the present day border between Hampshire and West Sussex will be found a collection of small villages and farms, which include the word 'marden' in their name, e.g. South Marden, Up Marden. Marden is an Old English word meaning border or boundary.

Another example of continuity, albeit a minor one, was revealed by recent excavations at Worthing, on the site of an old school in Little High Street. A boundary ditch was discovered: a ditch that had been dug first of all in Bronze Age times, and then re-dug regularly right up until the medieval period. Such evidence is not unique to Worthing, and is strongly suggestive of a continuous history, not one abruptly halted by invasion and massacre.

The Sussex Kings and the coming of Christianity

If we are to believe the chroniclers' description of Aella, as being a great military figure amongst the early English, it is perhaps surprising that nothing more is heard of him, or his sons, or even of his kingdom, for well over a hundred years. The reference we do find for the year 607 simply states that, "Ceolwulf fought the South Saxons." Ceolwulf was king of the West Saxons. By the seventh century it was becoming much more common to find the terms 'Sussex' and 'Wessex' being used to describe the kingdoms of respectively, the South Saxons and the West Saxons.

Another half century is to pass before we find mention again of Sussex, although there are numerous and increasingly detailed accounts of events in Wessex and Kent, Sussex's two most prominent neighbours. Wessex at this time was establishing itself as one of the most powerful of the English kingdoms, its territory ran from the Sussex border to the river Tamar; its only serious rival was the midlands kingdom of Mercia. Kent was also important, but for different reasons, for its success was based, not on territorial expansion, but on trade. By the late sixth century the burial goods being found in Kentish graves are of increasing superior quality, coming from many foreign lands. By contrast the burial goods found in Sussex graves of the period are drab and utilitarian, being generally locally produced. In the year 597 Kent converted to Christianity, thereby re-joining the 'civilised' world. Over the following decades all the English kingdoms converted, save one: Sussex.

It is indeed remarkable that the inhabitants of far away Northumbria were turned away from their pagan beliefs many years before the South Saxons. It is even more remarkable to consider that nearly a century separates the conversion of Kent, and the conversion of Sussex. How can this be explained? The answer almost certainly lies in the remoteness of the Sussex people from their neighbours. To the north the great forest of the Weald, over a hundred miles in length, and about twenty miles in width, closed off all communication. To the east, great areas of hazardous marshland divided Kent from Sussex, and similar conditions prevailed on the coast south and west of Chichester. Probably the safest and most reliable way of reaching the people of Sussex was by boat, which is indeed the method chosen by Wilfrid, Bishop of Ripon, when he came to bring Christianity to the South Saxons.

Before Wilfrid came there was more fighting. The ASC records the following for the year 661 -

"Wulfhere, son of Penda, ravaged the Isle of Wight and gave the inhabitants over to Aethelwalh, king of Sussex, because Wulfhere had received him at baptism."

Wulfhere was king of Mercia. This alliance between Mercia and Sussex momentarily wrong-footed Wessex, which was forced to cede territory, including the Isle of Wight and the area of the Meon valley to King Aethelwalh of Sussex. It would seem that Wulfhere's only condition was that Aethelwalh should convert to Christianity. However there is good reason to believe that this conversion was purely a ploy, and not undertaken with any sincerity. Indeed five years later Aethelwalh is apparently urging his kinsmen to kill Bishop Wilfrid and his monks when they land inadvertently on his shores.

The source for these claims is Eddius Stephenus, Wilfrid's biographer, although perhaps eulogiser would be a more appropriate word. Eddius was not attempting a critical analysis of Wilfrid's life and works. His is a religious work, designed to show the piety and spiritual resilience of Wilfrid: it is a work designed to inspire and give succour to the devout. So it is with some caution we should consider what is said and written about Sussex, its people and king.

According to Eddius, Wilfrid and his monks were forced by high winds onto sandbanks off the Sussex coast in year 666. Instead of being offered assistance, they encountered hostility. A pagan priest arrived, followed some time later by King Aethelwalh. According to Eddius the Sussex people would have killed Wilfrid and his monks, had not the Lord intervened, causing the tide to come in earlier than usual, Wilfrid's vessel was thereby raised from its sandbank, and the monks were able to escape. On the shore, standing on a mound, the pagan priest continued to hurl forth curses on the Christians, one of whom responded with a well aimed sling-shot, which felled and killed the pagan. So ended the first attempt to convert the South Saxons.

Wilfrid returned however, and this time he meant to stay. It is believed that a small Christian community, possibly of the Celtic as opposed to the Roman tradition, did exist at Bosham, and so long as they kept themselves to themselves they were unmolested by their pagan neighbours. Wilfrid however would settle for nothing less than the conversion of all the Sussex people. Fifteen years were to elapse before his arrival at Selsey in 681. According to Eddius the condition of the South Saxons was a grievous one: there was drought and famine, and men in groups of fifty were throwing themselves off high cliffs, presumably as a sacrificial offering to their gods.

The ancient Crypt at Bosham Church (WSCC)

Wilfrid stepped ashore, and for the first time in three years, down came the rains! He taught the men of Sussex how to fish with nets, and then showed them the way of the true faith. Well that's what Eddius says. It seems probable that the story is at least partly true. Despite, or perhaps because of Wilfrid, the omens were not good for Sussex. For the year 685, the ASC tells us that there was, "a bloody rain, and milk and butter turned to blood." The following year the forces of Wessex, led by their famous warrior king, Ceadwalla, over-ran Sussex. There is even a suspicion that Wilfrid, a friend of Ceadwalla was little more than a spy, and that his 'missionary' work was simply a reconnaissance for the planned invasion.

It is interesting to note that both the names Aethelwalh and Ceadwalla, are suggestive of Celtic as well as Saxon ancestry. This further suggests intermarriage and assimilation. However this is not an assimilation of equals. Britons, if they wanted to survive and prosper, had to adapt to English ways. Those Britons who stuck to the old culture were likely to persecuted and killed, and many became slaves. Others of course fled to West Wales, or Wales proper.

Ceadwalla was succeeded by another powerful king, Ine, who further strengthened the position of Wessex in southern England. The year 710 saw a campaign against the Britons of the west country, in which Nunna, described as being the king of Sussex and a 'kinsman' of Ine, took part. In the year 722 a series of rebellions broke across Wessex. In the west, Queen Aethelburg in concert with a nobleman called Ealdbriht, burned Taunton, while in the east the men of Sussex rose to re-assert their independence. During this period it is unclear as to whether Sussex came under one ruler, or several. There are references at this time to a "Wattus Rex", who may have been a king of Sussex, or simply the ruler of the area around Hastings. The "Haestingas" appear to have been a separate tribal grouping, being neither part of Sussex, nor part of Kent. Their origins are obscure, had they perhaps been pagan Jutes unwilling to accept Christianity, who had left Kent and established their own territory? What is known is that as recently as the nineteenth century the dialect of the Hastings area was quite distinct from that spoken in either Kent or East Sussex.

We also know that at this time there were two king-like figures operating in Sussex. One, Byrthun was in control of the western part of Sussex, the other, Andhun, in the east. This suggests that the division of our present day county into 'West' and 'East' Sussex is far older than some people imagine. It is also possible that even at this early stage, Chichester or Selsey was the western capital, while Lewes was the main town in the east, with the Hastings area being a third division. In 725, having crushed the rebellion in the west country, Ine turned on Sussex. Ealdbriht had fled to the land of Byrthun, and both were killed in the subsequent battle. It follows therefore that the western part of Sussex was re-conquered at this time, but it is less certain what became of the land held by Andhun.

By the later eighth century it was Mercia, rather than Wessex, which was in the ascendancy, under King Offa, regarded by some as the first true ruler of all the English. At this time Sussex appears to have been ruled by Oslac, whose power was clearly subordinate to that of Offa. When Oslac granted land he could only do so with the endorsement of Offa. Oslac was therefore a 'client' king. After Offa's death the tables were turned, and both Sussex and Kent came back under the control of Wessex, after which time no more is heard of a Sussex king, although the 'duces' of Sussex remain important figures.

Later Saxon Sussex and the Norman Conquest

By the late eighth century, the English were emerging as more of a unified nation, although the land was still divided into three distinct kingdoms: Wessex, Mercia, and Northumbria. Sussex of course came under the jurisdiction of Wessex. At a time when people could have hoped for peace and stability, they were faced by invasion, from the 'Viking' forces of Scandinavia. The Anglo-Saxon Chronicle for 793 vividly evokes the terror of those days-

"In this year fierce, foreboding omens came over the land of Northumbria, and wretchedly terrified the people. There were excessive whirlwinds, lightning storms, and fiery dragons were seen flying in the sky. These signs were followed by great famine, and shortly after in the same year, on 8 January, the ravaging of heathen men destroyed God's church at Lindisfarne through brutal robbery and slaughter."

It was only a matter of time before the Vikings made their way into southern England. Indeed by the late ninth century, all of Northumbria, East Anglia, and most of Mercia was under Viking control. Had it not been for the charismatic and inspired leadership of Alfred the Great (King of Wessex, and acknowledged King of all the English), the whole nation might have succumbed. It was in Alfred's reign that great fortresses, known as 'Burghs' were constructed across south-east England, including Sussex. At Lewes, Chichester, and Burpham, large earth embankments were raised, and the local population made ready for resistance.

In 894 the ASC describes how the Vikings "ravaged up in Sussex near Chichester", it also explains that the Danish force was routed by the men of Sussex, who, "put them to flight, killed many thousands of them, and seized some of their ships." Unlike the early entries in the ASC, the events described in Alfred's reign are believed to have been written down as they happened, or not long afterwards, thereby giving greater validity to the details they contain. Certainly if "many thousands" had perished at the battle near Chichester it would have been a great blow for the Danish invaders, and therefore a great victory for the English.

About five or six miles north of Chichester, in a valley, which even to this day is both remote and unspoiled, is an area of woodland which contains a cluster of ancient yew trees, believed by many to be the oldest trees in the county. According to legend they were planted by the victorious Saxons to mark their defeat over the Danes. Anyone visiting Kingly Vale, particularly on a late afternoon in autumn will sense a certain atmosphere, centred around these gnarled and massive old trees, and by the stillness of their surroundings. This dark enclave of yew and oak, illuminated by the dappled light of the waning sun, lends itself to flights of the imagination, where the long dead spirits of ancient conflicts may appear in the rustle of leaves on the forest floor, or in the lengthening shadows of the dying day.

Burpham owes its existence and its name (the settlement by the Burgh) to the Anglo-Danish wars. After the danger passed, Burpham remained an important place for the South Saxons. Even today, a visit to its surprisingly large parish church will confirm its former status. The church, despite several periods of rebuilding and restoration still contains Saxon workmanship. It was the Normans who, after 1066, keen to establish their own centres of power and control, sidelined Burpham and created a new town and castle, on the other side of the river at Arundel.

After the great victories of Alfred's grandson, Athelstan (924-939), all the Viking possessions in this country were returned to English control, and gradually peace and order were restored. This 'golden age' of the Saxon era reached its height during the reign of Edgar (959-975), suitably known as 'the Peaceable'. It was then that men and women, *Sompting Church 1850 (WSCC)*

undistracted by the demands of war and conflict, could divert their energies into cultural and spiritual efforts. It was at this time that Sussex's surviving Saxon churches were built (earlier buildings had been made of wood). There is the round-towered church at Southease, near Seaford; the church of Sompting, with its famous 'rhenish helm', mimicking many of the churches seen to this day in northern Germany; the Romanesque church at Worth, very different in design from all others in the county; and the church of St. Nicholas at Old Shoreham, described by the late Enoch Powell as one of the best surviving examples of Anglo-Saxon architecture anywhere in the country.

The good times did not last however. Edgar's successor, Edward, was murdered at Corfe. He was followed by the Ethelred, famous as the 'Unready', or more correctly, the 'unread', or the unwise. During his reign, which tragically for the English lasted the thirty-eight years from 978 till 1016, invasion and war returned. The Vikings came again, well armed and in large numbers. Buoyed up by the prosperity of previous reigns, Ethelred tried to buy peace with 'Danegeld'. However his policy of giving the invaders gold to go away only encouraged them to return, seeking more rich pickings. Eventually Ethelred, fearful of losing all his possessions, ordered the slaughter of all Danes or those of Danish extraction living within his realm. This terrible blood-letting, which led to Ethelred being described as the 'evil counselled' king, was to have an even worse conclusion.

On learning that his own sister had been among those massacred, Swain, King of Denmark, ordered an invasion of England in which vengeance, not gold, would be the prime motive. As the Viking armies swept across England, they gave no mercy. It was said that sightless, defiled bodies were piled high. At this juncture, Ethelred fled the country, and sought sanctuary in Normandy. In Normandy he married Emma, sister of Richard, Duke of Normandy. They had two sons, Alfred and Edward, who although of the Saxon line, were brought up in exile in Normandy. Back in England, Ethelred's eldest son by his first marriage, Edmund, now took up the war against the Danes. He enjoyed success, and was called 'Edmund Ironside' by the English, who unfavourably contrasted his military prowess with that of his father.

Finally, in 1016, Ethelred died, and at twenty-two Edmund became king, to general acclamation. However before the year was out, he too would be dead, killed by the combined effects of desease and exhaustion. Also dead was Swain, king of the Danes. In order to save further loss of life, and because there was no other obvious or acceptable candidate, the earls of England 'elected' Swain's son, Canute (or Cnut as it is now usually spelt) as their new king. It is now that Godwin, Earl of Wessex steps centre stage, for it is he who becomes the new king's most trusted English advisor. It is no coincidence that so many legends concerning Cnut (the turning back of the waves, the burial of his young daughter), should be set at Bosham, home of Earl Godwin.

From this moment on, until the great battle near Hastings in 1066, the

Godwin family of Sussex is the most important family in the realm, and increasingly so as the years go by. In Sussex in particular, the people show great loyalty and allegiance to them and their cause. And what was their cause? Put simply it was to ensure that foreign influence, be it Danish or Norman, should be resisted, while as much power as possible resided with Englishmen, or to be specific, with Earl Godwin. Godwin ensured that he was the new king's principal advisor, and eventually his only advisor. Even Cnut's Danish kinsmen failed to enjoy the influence that Godwin achieved. Cnut declared that he wished his reign to take its impulse from that of the revered and lamented King Edgar. Indeed Cnut adopted with enthusiasm the English traditions of his new kingdom.

When Cnut died in 1035, Godwin plotted and connived to ensure that the next king would be amenable to an 'English' policy. When Alfred (eldest son of Ethelred and Emma of Normandy) arrived to put his claim to the throne, he was mysteriously kidnapped, and later murdered. Godwin is generally believed to have been responsible for this crime. In quick succession, two of Cnut's sons succeeded to the throne, but both were dead before their twenty-fifth birthdays (apparently dying of natural causes). With no other heirs left to procure, Godwin was forced to accept Ethelred's last son, Edward as king in 1042. Edward, known as 'the Confessor', was not only pious, he was also heavily influenced by his Norman upbringing. Godwin was horrified, and together with his sons, vowed to reverse this shift in their fortunes.

The Godwins and their Sussex kinsmen had a reputation for wild and reckless behaviour. However, when Godwin's eldest son, Swain, murdered one of the king's nephews in a drunken brawl, and then seduced an Abbess, Edward decided to act. Encouraged by his Norman advisors, the king declared Swain to be 'nithing', that is a man without honour, and he was banished. When his father and brothers rose in his defence, they were outlawed, and fled abroad. This appeared to be a triumph for the Norman party, and the end for the Godwins. However the people of Sussex remained loyal to their Earl. When Godwin returned from exile, with his sons, and a mercenary army, the people of Sussex flocked to his banner, and together they marched on London.

The King had an army, and London was well defended. He could also hope to rely on military support from Normandy. All his hopes were to be dashed however: the Londoners refused to fight Godwin. Humiliated and vulnerable, the king capitulated. Godwin entered the capital in triumph. Godwin and his English party had gained complete control of the kingdom. King Edward now largely turned his back on the world, and devoted himself to matters of religion. True to form Swain was killed in a drunken brawl, while the following year, Godwin himself, goblet in hand, collapsed and died at a banquet. Power now passed to his second son, Harold, always famous as the English king, killed at Hastings by an arrow in the eye. It is important to realise that although Harold was only officially king for less than one year, in reality he exercised the power of a king from the time of his father's death in 1052, fourteen years before the Battle of Hastings.

Those fourteen years were good ones for Sussex. Harold was popular throughout the realm, but the origin of his power was in Sussex, something he was keenly aware of. His authority was not God-given, but arose from the common will of the people. When the saintly, and increasingly hermit-like Edward the Confessor died, shortly after consecrating Westminster Abbey, during the Christmas of 1065, the people looked to Harold to be their new king. To the English there was no doubt about the succession, but in truth, Harold had no right to be king. Two others had a far better claim: Harold Hardrada, King of Norway, and a descendant of Cnut; and William, Duke of Normandy, whose great aunt, Emma, had been married to Ethelred. William had also been close to Edward, who, it is said, had promised the throne of England to him.

The English would have none of this. There was a new confidence in the land. Hardrada, the last of the great Viking warrior kings was a formidable foe, but he could be vanquished. As for William, few rated his chances, and many may have wondered if he would even dare to risk an invasion.

Hardrada came first. At Fulford Bridge he defeated the northern earls, but at the subsequent battle at Stamford Bridge, near York, he was surprised by the speedy arrival of Harold and his fighting men from the south. In a brutal battle, in which many were killed, the last Viking invasion of England was defeated, and Hardrada was killed. No sooner had victory been secured than news reached Harold that William had landed in Sussex, and without waiting to draw breath, Harold marched south. On entering London he was urged to wait for reinforcements, and to secure the more easily defendable North Downs rather than meet William in Sussex. But Harold had all the impetuous qualities and

A romanticised, 19th century view of the Battle of Hastings (WSCC)

hot temper of the Godwins. He would not wait while 'William the Bastard' stood upon the soil of Sussex. Harold marched south, where he was met by the Sussex militia or 'fyrd'.

On Saturday, 14 October 1066, Harold set his standard on a ridge of rising ground close to the hamlet of Senlac, north of Hastings. William, with his French and Breton allies marched to engage him (and here is a touch of irony, for the Bretons were of course descendants of the Britons, displaced by the Saxons some six centuries earlier). The battle lasted eight hours, about four times the length of most such conflicts at that time. The Normans had superior technology (archery, chain-mailed knights etc.), and better generalship. The English had the cause of national survival to sustain them, and a particular loyalty to the house of Godwin. Much has been written of how the Normans tricked the English into believing they were retreating, while in reality they were luring them into an ambush. Such stories were written by the victors. None-the-less defeat did ensue for the English, and when it came it was absolute. Some scholars have even doubted if any of the English survived the rout. Harold was killed, so were all his brothers, and his kinsmen. The Normans had taken their revenge for the humiliation of 1052. Never again would an Englishman sit on the throne of England. As an everlasting memorial to his victory, William endowed an abbey at the scene of his triumph, around which the town of 'Battle' would develop. Battle Abbey actually stands on the very ridge on which Harold and his men perished in 1066.

England was stunned by the defeat. In desperation the people tried to find an explanation for such a dire turn of events, which had handed them over to the rule of a foreign prince. The chroniclers were very clear as to the reasons, they even rebuked the surviving English nobles for continuing the resistance to William, instead of going and paying him homage. "They went at need, when the most harm was done," says the ASC, "and it was most unwise that no one had gone before, as God would not amend it for our sins." In other words the Almighty had punished the people for allowing Harold, a man with no God-given right to be king, to sit on the English throne. William, on the other hand did have a rightful claim, and unlike Harold he was a great benefactor of the Church.

England was cowed by William. For centuries the people were forced to yield to the 'Norman Yoke', and to all the feudal system represented. However if 1066 proved a disaster for England as a whole, it was little short of a catastrophe for Sussex. This county was treated with greater severity than any of its neighbours. William was keenly aware that Sussex was the land of the Godwins, and that its people were potentially his greatest foes. Following Hastings, Norman knights traversed the county from east to west, burning, killing and despoiling. So great was the trail of destruction, that twenty years later, the value of the land along this route was still very low compared to the surrounding districts. All the land previously held by Saxons was seized, and transferred to Norman control. Only in Sussex was such a total sequestration of Saxon assets undertaken.

William then granted the administrative divisions, known as 'rapes' in Sussex to his Norman kinsmen. The rape of Hastings he gave to his father's cousin, the Count of Eu; Robert de Mortain was granted Pevensey; Lewes went to William de Warrene; Bramber to William de Braose; and Arundel, by far the largest district, was granted to Roger de Montgomery, who was also given the title, Earl of Sussex. These Barons were, subject to the King's grace, masters of all they surveyed. In order to ensure control over their new domains, they built stone castles in prominent positions, usually by strategic rivers. More than this, they created new towns, in order that the

The remains of William & Gundrada de Warrene, discovered in 1845 (WSCC)

Saxon centres of power should be marginalised. Arundel replaced Burpham in the west. Bramber was the Norman substitute for Steyning. In the east of the county, Battle, and its increasingly powerful and wealthy abbey became a centre for Norman power and control. Even the ecclesiastical arrangements were altered. Wilfrid's cathedral at Selsey, a humble wooden structure, was abandoned, and a new cathedral was built at Chichester. To emphasise the new order, the Normans constructed their cathedral largely of Caen limestone, shipped over from Normandy. The port to which most of these Norman materials came was Shoreham, and even here the conquerors built the town of New Shoreham, to replace the old Saxon settlement.

In many respects the seal was now set on Sussex for the next seven or eight hundred years. Only with the transport revolution of the late eighteenth and early nineteenth century, did the pattern of life begin to change dramatically in Sussex. The descendants of the Norman lords were as entrenched in 1766 as they had been in 1066. It is known that Richard Fitzalan, Earl of Arundel in the fourteenth century, had massive holdings of land in Sussex. These included 64 manors, twelve forests, thirteen deer parks, 13,000 acres of arable land, and 10,000 acres of woodland. Even at the end of the last century, the 15th Duke of Norfolk still held sway over a large part of West Sussex, in much the same way as his predecessors. Most people in the rural areas, directly or indirectly owed their livelihood to the Duke, rented their cottage from the Duke, and looked to Arundel castle for governance and justice. The long term ramifications for the county of Sussex of the Norman Conquest, were therefore immense.

ARUNDEL & THE ARUN VALLEY

"Since William rose and Harold fell, there have been Earls at Arundel," so says a popular local rhyme, which in essence sums up the history of this town. Arundel would have been of little importance without its Earls, in fact it might never have come into existence at all. The first Earl, Roger de Montgomery was a kinsman of William the Conqueror, and it was he who established the castle at Arundel, and the town that later grew around it. Prior to the conquest it was Burpham, on the other side of the River Arun that was the significant local settlement, but the Normans tried wherever possible in Sussex to supplant Saxon cultural centres with those of their own (see p......). In other words Arundel was a Norman 'new town', and a symbol of Norman power. The Montgomery line eventually passed to the Fitzalan line, and then to the Howards, who had the title 'Duke of Norfolk' bestowed on them. All power lay with the Duke at the castle, and this power remained pervasive until recent times. Writing in 1903, E V Lucas still detected this influence, and the town's prevailing 'foreignness'-

" I know of no town with so low a pulse as this precipitous little settlement under the shadow of Rome and the Duke. In spite of picnic parties in the park, in spite of anglers from London, in spite of the railway in the valley, Arundel is still medieval and curiously foreign. On a very hot day, as one climbs the hill to the cathedral, one might be in old France, and certainly in the Middle Ages."

E V Lucas (WSCC)

The 'shadow of Rome' is a reference to the unbroken Catholicism of the Dukes. Even during the most zealous phase of the Reformation, they would not renounce the Faith. Sir Philip Howard conspired with foreign envoys, in the hope of restoring the old order, and ended up in the Tower of London as a result. Yet the Howards regained their possessions, and although they did not incline again to treason, they never wavered in their religious convictions. So Arundel became an island of Roman Catholicism in an often raging sea of Protestantism. During the civil war, the family took refuge overseas. On three occasions in little over a year, rival armies pillaged the town, and besieged the castle (see p81). No other town in Sussex suffered at that time as Arundel suffered.

Arundel 1798 (WSCC)

During the eighteenth century the Duke became not just the most prominent Catholic in the county, but also the main champion of the Tory Party. Yet for most of the eighteenth century the Tories were out of power, and the Whigs governed. Elections were few and far between and notoriously corrupt. When the Duke's neighbours, the Shelleys of Mitchelgrove, renounced their Catholicism and their Toryism, and embraced the Whig cause and the Anglican Church, it was bad enough, but when they then proceeded to nominate Whig candidates, against the Duke's Tories, in the 1784 elections, it was treachery indeed. The George became the Tory headquarters in the town, while The Crown, on the other side of the High Street became the offices of the Whigs. Elections in those days lasted for forty days, although the electorate was minuscule. Voting was a public affair, in which men declared on the hustings for whom they would vote. Bribery and intimidation were rife. On this occasion, one Tory and one Whig were elected at Arundel. The Duke eventually re-established Arundel as a Tory stronghold, and his heirs took a direful revenge on the Shelleys old home at Michelgrove.

Arundel Castle was badly damaged during the civil war, and left in a state of dilapidation for seventy years, until the eighth Duke began rebuilding. This process was continued by the eleventh Duke, who also diverted the London Road, thereby giving greater privacy to his new quarters. This Duke was rich and powerful, and also somewhat eccentric. He kept and bred owls, which nested in the old Norman keep. Getting some of the owls to breed proved troublesome, and ensuring that the subsequent eggs hatched was even more difficult. To the Duke, all the owls had personalities, so he named them after his friends, most of whom were very prominent men of the day. On one occasion, during a banquet, a servant rushed into the hall, bringing the Duke good news, to the stunned silence of the guests, he proclaimed, "Please, your Grace, Lord Thurlow has laid an egg." The real Lord Thurlow was Lord Chancellor of England at the time. The owl of the same name outlived his renowned namesake, and died at a great age in 1859.

It was the fifteenth Duke who created modern Arundel. Between 1867 and 1902, he rebuilt not just the town, but the castle as well. It was said that he was the richest man in England, a wealth that flowed not from his agricultural holdings in Sussex, but from his coal mines in Northumberland. His first great project was the cathedral, although until 1965 it only had the status of a church. It is of course a Catholic cathedral, and therefore does not bestow city status on Arundel. It was never truly completed. Designed by Hansom (more famous today for the cab he designed), the original plans show the cathedral with a great spire, which was to stand on the truncated tower in the north-west corner. However as the construction neared completion, a group of local surveyors, tactfully approached the Duke, warning of the possible consequences if the spire were built. The building would be top-heavy they said, and gravity would eventually force the entire building down the hill. The Duke relented, and so the church was left unfinished.

The Duke turned his attention to other, smaller buildings: the Post Office (once the largest in the county), the shops on the eastern side of the High Street, buildings in Maltravers Street - all built in an old style, but all really late Victorian. Then came the castle. He would build the biggest and the best medieval castle in the county, if not in the country, except of course it would not really be medieval. For years and years men worked on the project, great curtain walls arose, turrets emerged, and battlements were constructed across the roof of the earlier building. Not until 1902 was the work completed. Sadly the visitor to Arundel, who remarks on the fine preservation of the old castle, has to be gently told that most of what they see is nineteenth century, and some is even, (if only just), twentieth century.

Some real medieval ruins stand by the river. They are all that remains of the Blackfriars monastery, although for many years they were mistakenly identified as being the remains of the Maison Dieu, or charity hospital, founded by Richard Fitzalan, sixth Earl of Arundel in the 1390's. This Earl plotted against King Richard II, and was responsible for the downfall and subsequent execution of many of the King's favourites in 1389. Ten years later, the King, having conspired long and meticulously, moved against the Earl and his supporters. Richard Fitzalan was arrested and executed. Not long after, another plot brought about the King's downfall and murder, and chief amongst the conspirators was the son of the beheaded Earl of Arundel. Such was the price of political intrigue in the fourteenth century.

In the earlier quote from Lucas, mention was made of anglers coming down from London for the fishing. Mullet was the main catch in this stretch of the Arun, and Arundel people were known by the same name, in fact they still are! To be a 'Mullet' is a source of great pride, and increasingly rare as well, for the only stipulation is that the aspirant must be born in Arundel - not so common since the Arundel Hospital closed some thirty years ago.

Burpham has been rediscovered in recent years. Go there on a day in summer, and you will find the car-park by the cricket ground overflowing with cars. The George and Dragon will be bursting with customers, and in every direction groups of walkers will be heading up into the hills, or down by the river. Yet go there on a bleak day in winter, and all is silent. Few cars pass you by, for the road ends at Burpham, and visitors are few and far between at that time of year. It was this very peace and tranquillity which attracted so many artists and writers to Burpham a century ago, when the village's slow

Arundel 1846 (WSCC)

33

pace of life was only ever disturbed by the annual sheep dipping in the Arun. John Cowper Powys, John Ruskin and Mervyn Peake, all found escape from city life at Burpham. In 1898, Tickner Edwardes, then a successful journalist came to Burpham, and remained until his death in 1944. Edwardes took holy orders late in life, and was vicar of Burpham between 1927 and 1935. In his books and articles he lovingly chronicled the life of the village for nearly half a century.

Burpham originated as one of Alfred the Great's forts or 'burgh's', built to defend southern England against the Viking raiders (see p25) Today the cricket and recreation ground stand on the old fort, which took full advantage of this natural land promontory. A high earth bank was raised to the north, and is still clearly visible today (the entrance to the car-park cuts through it). After 1066, Burpham was eclipsed by Arundel, and remained an obscure sheep-farming community until recent times. In his last book, 'A Downland Year', published in 1939, Tickner Edwardes offers several glimpses of village life, which could have been just as easily written in 1839, or perhaps even earlier, such as this description of oat threshing and bed-making -

"They are threshing oats in the rick-yard on this wind-wild morning, and across the yard there is a great careering drift of something that, from a little distance, looks like smoke.

It is the dust and finer particles of the chaff that the wind carries farthest. Much of this does not settle in the yard at all, but goes soaring up over the barn-roof and across the meadows in a long cloud-streamer that the sun riddles through and through with gold. The lighter husks, the 'fliers', as countryfolk call them, are gathering in a pale yellow drift under the rick-yard wall; and there an old woman is busy stuffing armfuls of them into a bed-case pillow of snow-white linen. She will trundle it home presently on the ancient perambulator that stands by, and it will serve her for bed until oat-threshing-time comes round again. A chaff-bed is, in point of fact, as softly comfortable as any bed of feathers, only it must be filled with genuine wind-winnowed oat-fliers and changed at every fall."

Incidentally 'fall' was the country word for 'autumn' long before the first colonist had set foot in America. Not all the literary persons who came to Burpham blended in as well as Tickner Edwardes. John Cowper Powys, for instance, had a house in the village (Warre House, now known as Frith House) that backed onto the burgh, and he was often disturbed by local youths clambering about on the embankment as he was trying to work in his study. In order to stop the nuisance, he erected a sign on the bank, declaring, 'Trespassers will be Prosecuted.' The indignant locals tore it down, and when Powys put up a second sign, that too ended up in the ditch. His irreligious views did not go down well in this conservative little community, and even his own wife was embarrassed by his behaviour.

John Ruskin used to spend his summers at near-by Peppering, and found total relaxation amongst the high hills of Sussex, where only the sound of sheep bells disturbed the natural sounds of nature. Mervyn Peake lies buried in Burpham churchyard, as does the saintly Tickner Edwardes. Peake's father was the village Doctor, and lived at Reed Thatch in Wepham. On the outbreak of World War II, Mervyn enlisted, but his health which had always been poor did not benefit from military life, and he suffered a mental breakdown. He was discharged from the army, and during the winter of 1940-41, he came with his wife and young son back to Burpham. The family stayed initially in a dismal cottage at Warningcamp, which looked out over the watermeadows to Arundel Castle. Peake was sure the cottage was haunted, while the battlements of the castle, rising grey and forbidding over the winter landscape, activated his imagination and formed the basis for Gormenghast Castle, and the 'Titus' trilogy of novels that were to make him famous. He later moved to '94 Wepham,' the cottage next to Reed Thatch, and remained there till the end of the war. He found work in Brighton, where he taught illustration at the Brighton College of Art. He died of Parkinson's Disease in 1968.

Burpham churchyard has many interesting memorials. Next to the church porch is the grave of the eighteenth century jockey, Ben Brewster, who won the Derby on three occasions. Just by the path that leads northwards through the churchyard, is the grave of Mary Goble, and her brother, Moses. Curiously it faces west, while most of the other headstones face east. A strange tale surrounds Mary Goble. In the 1850's a French maid in her employ disappeared, and was never seen again. Local gossip claimed she had been murdered by 'Madam Goble.' So persistent was this belief that, even after her death, naughty children in the village could always be made to pay attention by their parents' reminder that "Madam Goble walks." This ominous, yet unspecific threat kept many an anxious child awake at night.

Buried next to Tickner Edwardes, is another vicar of Burpham, Hermen Schnieder, who became Canon of Jerusalem. A Jew, who converted to Christianity, Schnieder was the only member of his family to escape the Nazi persecution in Germany. On coming to this country, he was taken in by a Christian family, who ensured that he was brought up and educated in the Jewish faith. At University he converted to Christianity, and devoted his life to the cause of Jewish/ Christian understanding, and became a special advisor to the Archbishop of Canterbury.

Three miles north of Burpham is **Amberley**, with its 'castle', which was actually built as a fortified manor house for the Bishop of Chichester (see p46). Just as Arundel people were known as 'Mullets', so Amberley folk were known as 'Trouts', although the name has not survived, perhaps because the retired city folk who now live there, did not fancy being known as 'Old Trouts'. The former chalk quarry has been converted into an open air museum of industrial archaeology that is well worth a visit.

Littlehampton has little to offer in the way of historic or literary interest. Until 1930 the entire town was owned by the Duke of Norfolk, who in that year sold it to a development company . Very quickly some of the town's most historic landmarks were destroyed, including the old windmill, coastguard cottages, and 'pepper-pot' lighthouse that stood at the harbour entrance. South Terrace is Regency, and still quite attractive, as are parts of New Road, however crass developments in the 1960's and 70's damaged the architectural integrity of the area. The old Beach Hotel which stood on the Common was recently demolished to make way for luxury apartments. Amidst the mud and silt of Littlehampton Harbour, it is still possible to find relics from the D-Day landings, including at least one motor-torpedo boat, and several landing craft.

Climping is to be found on the west bank of the river. Its church is very fine indeed, with a magnificent dog-tooth archway. Buried in the churchyard is Lord Moyne, formerly Arthur Guinness, who was assassinated in Cairo in 1944 by Jewish nationalists. Moyne lived at Bailiffscourt, now an exclusive hotel. Visitors may be surprised to learn that most of the buildings, with the exception of the old chapel were built during the 1920's and 30's, but using old materials. Other buildings in the grounds, such as the old granary were transported by Moyne from other parts of the country.

North of Climping, and west of Arundel is **Slindon**, the childhood home of

Bailiffscourt in 1914

Hilaire Belloc, who lived here in the 1870's and 80's. The village, formerly owned by the Newburgh family is now in the ownership of the National Trust, who ensure that the old houses and cottages are kept in a good state of preservation. The Trust have recently opened a 'bothy' for Downs walkers wanting a cheap overnight stop. In the parish church is one of only a handful of surviving wooden grave effigies. It represents Anthony St. Leger, a squire, during the reign of Henry VII. The effigy fascinated the young Belloc, who wrote the following poem in its honour-

There is no name upon his grave
If his grave it haps to be
And his face doth look towards the plain
And towards the calm blue sea.
He lies in a quiet church aisle
With the small churchyard in view
By a little Gothic window
And 'neath a shadowy yew.
He may have been carved for ages
And oft heard the tolling bell
And he may lie for ages more there

In that church aisle - who can tell?
There is no name upon his grave
If his grave it haps to be
And his face doth look towards the plain
And towards the calm blue sea.

Not an outstanding poem, you may think, but pretty impressive for a nine year old!

There is also a memorial in the church to Archbishop Stephen Langton, who died at Slindon in 1228, and is famous for standing up to King John, and persuading him to sign the Magna Carta in 1215.

On Nore Hill is a ruined archway. It was built as a folly for the Countess of Newburgh in 1815, who was keen to provide employment for local men returning home from the wars. Close by is Courthill Farm, where Hilaire Belloc stayed on his return to Slindon in 1905, after many foreign adventures. He later wrote of his home-coming, which he found a deeply moving experience -

Nore Hill Folly

"The many things that I recovered as I came up the countryside were not less charming than when a distant memory had enshrined them, but much more. Whatever veil is thrown by a longing recollection had not intensified nor even made more mysterious the beauty of that happy ground; nor in my very dreams of morning had I, in exile, seen it more beloved or more rare. Much also that I had forgotten now returned to me as I approached - a group of elms, a little turn of the parson's wall, a small paddock beyond the graveyard close, cherished by one man, with a low wall of very old stone guarding it all round. And all these things fulfiled and amplified my delight, till even the good vision of the place, which I had kept so many years, left me and was replaced by its better reality. 'Here,' I said to myself, 'is a symbol of what some say is reserved for the soul: pleasure of a kind which cannot be imagined save in the moment when at last it is attained."

Another curious Sussex folly, is the Toat Monument at **Pulborough**. This solitary tower was constructed during the early nineteenth century, and its originally purpose is obscure. One legend states that it was lived in for a number of years by a 'prisoner', who never left its confines, and was passed food and water by means of a small flap in the locked doorway. His imprisonment was part of an experiment to ascertain the effects of sensory deprivation of both mind and body. When the poor man was at last released, he had long straggling hair, and fingernails that measured over a foot in length. The more mundane explanation that it was built so the local landowner could view the sea from his estates, is perhaps more likely to be closer to the truth.

WORTHING, SHOREHAM, & THE ADUR VALLEY

Worthing's literary visitors at the turn of the century were none too complimentary about the town. Augustus Hare commented, "It is a very ugly, uninteresting place," but, he conceded, it did have, "a relaxing climate," and "pleasant excursions may be made from it." W H Hudson, who actually owned a house in Bedford Row, wrote scathingly, "I hate the place and have never met anyone in it who has been of use to me. It is talk, talk, talk, but never a gleam of an original or fresh remark or view of anything that does not come out of a book or newspaper." In his book, 'The Four Men,' Hilaire Belloc tells of a ghost that haunted a house at Dial Post, and how the wanton spirit was exorcised to the "Marine Parade at Worthing, where no one minded him." However Virginia Wolfe had a nice time here, and Oscar Wilde enjoyed his stay in the town, where he wrote his famous play, 'The Importance of Being Earnest." Richard Jefferies, on the other hand can hardly have been said to have enjoyed his short stay at Goring (now a suburb of Worthing), for he died there in 1887, at the early age of thirty-eight.

Worthing grew-up in the wake of Brighton, following a visit to the town by Princess Amelia in 1798. Over the next half century, hundreds of people moved into the town from the rural hinterland, seeking employment in the service sector, which was so vital to the success of a seaside resort. The railway came to Worthing in 1845, and the pier (a sure mark of a successful resort) was opened in 1862. In 1890 the town was incorporated, and twelve years later the neighbouring villages of Broadwater and Tarring were added to the borough, followed in 1929 by Goring and Durrington. The population of Worthing today stands at 100,000, making it the largest town in West Sussex, and the second largest in Sussex as a whole, after Brighton. Yet despite its size, Worthing lacks either a significant historic quarter, nor one that is modern and vibrant. Most of the town's best old buildings were demolished between 1958 and 1970 in an orgy of unimaginative re-development. The present day 'white elephants,' the Guildbourne Centre and the Teville Gate complex, stand as dreary epitaphs

Montague Place, Worthing C.1925 (WSCC)

to past mistakes. The old Town Hall, and an almost unique Georgian theatre were sacrificed on the alter of short-term expediency. Sadly, Worthing is still paying the price, although the recent pedestrianisation scheme has helped lift the mood. It is a pity that these improvements have been somewhat marred by the erection of unsightly, expensive (and to this author's mind), wholly unnecessary observation cameras. 'CCTV' is, however flavour of the month, and no one is allowed to speak a word against it.

There are historic buildings to be found in the town, some of which owe their survival to Eric Cockain, a former Conservation Officer, employed by the council, who turned conservation in Worthing into something of a crusade. The most historic street in the Borough is without a doubt, Tarring High Street. Of

Outside Worthing Old Town Hall - 1855 (WSCC)

especial interest is the 'Parsonage Restaurant', a timber framed building that dates back to the reign of Henry VI. Around the corner, in Glebe Road is the Bishop's Palace, a stone-built medieval building, and one of only two grade 1 listed buildings in the Borough (the other being Castle Goring, on the A27, Arundel Road). Castle Goring was once owned by the Shelley family, who also owned Mitchelgrove at **Patching**, which was demolished on the orders of the Duke of Norfolk (see p32) Patching wood was once famous for its truffles. These delicacies were unearthed by men with specially trained dogs. Pigs were also found to be highly gifted in the detection of the truffles, unfortunately they were also very partial to them, and considerable skill was required on the part of the truffle-hunter, to seize the fungi as soon as it was revealed, and before the pig had a chance to eat it first.

A truffle hunter with Sussex Spaniel dogs (WSCC)

Shoreham has suffered, but not to the same extent as Worthing. The main damage occurred here between the two World Wars. In 1923, the highly ornamental and visually pleasing, Norfolk Suspension Bridge, erected nearly a century earlier, was replaced by an horrific steel-girder bridge, which, mercifully, was itself replaced by an unimaginative, but inoffensive successor in 1987. The High Street was a very special place until 1938, with many very ancient buildings, including a Market house, around which traffic had to manoeuvre. However it was a street designed for localised, horse-drawn traffic, not for the increasing number of motor cars, making their way along the A259 to Brighton. Despite protests, from among others, Hilaire Belloc, the street was widened, and the old buildings pulled down. Unlike Worthing, were the cull of the old and architecturally interesting buildings was almost total, much still remains at Shoreham, and more than the passing motorist would probably realise.

Shoreham is actually two places - 'New Shoreham,' which began life as a thriving Norman port (see p30), and 'Old Shoreham', which may have been one of the first Saxon towns in Sussex, possibly pre-dating New Shoreham by as much as five hundred years or more. Old Shoreham is to the north, its fine old Saxon church stands close to the river, with the old wooden toll bridge (now a bridge for walkers) to the west, and the historic Red Lion Inn, to the south. The Victorian pub, "The Swiss Cottage," was once the gateway to a nineteenth century pleasure garden, with an ornamental lake. This lake was fashioned out of the remains of the original harbour. The current landlord of the Swiss Cottage has created a small museum of historic artefacts, found in the lake in recent years. The town's official museum is situated in the Marlipins, an early medieval customs house, situated in the High Street, and probably the oldest, non-ecclesiastical, stone building in Sussex. Opposite the Marlipins is the Crown and Anchor, which at the time of writing is painted a deathly black, this inn is said to have had many smuggling associations. The fine carved figure head is about seventy years old, and was carved out of one solid piece of wood, which replaced an earlier effigy that had become old and rotten. Shoreham's finest building is St. Mary's, the parish church of New Shoreham. It is as big as a Priory church, and as grand as a cathedral. It was once even larger (fragments of masonry can be found, covered with ivy in the west of the churchyard), but part of it was abandoned as the town declined, due to the silting up of the harbour.

Shoreham, historically was a frontier town. It may have stood between Britons and Saxons once, it has long stood between the contrasting destinies of East and West Sussex. As a port, it served both parts of the county, and was especially important to the settlements of central Sussex. It was said that the last significant smuggling run in Sussex came ashore at Shoreham in 1855, destined for a warehouse at Cuckfield.

Bramber is by modern standards a small village, but it was once of great importance. The Normans built a castle here, and William de Braose was its lord. The civil war left the castle a ruin (see p83), and the one great wall of the keep is everything a ruined castle should be: dramatic, brooding, and romantic. The village was, until 1832 a borough, which meant that it returned two Members of Parliament, even though the population by 1832 was less than one hundred. Bramber was one of the notorious 'pocket boroughs,' and it sat firmly in the pocket of the Duke of Norfolk, who ensured that both its members served the Tory interest in Parliament. One of those members was the anti-slavery campaigner, William Wilberforce. There is a story of Wilberforce passing through Bramber on a long journey, and being quite surprised to find himself in his own constituency, a place he had only visited on one previous occasion.

As well as the castle and the church, St. Mary's, a timber-framed house is well worth a visit. It is still a private residence, but is open two afternoons a week in the summer.

It was once the home of monks, charged with collecting tolls from travellers using the bridge, and ensuring it was kept in a good state of repair.

Until fairly recent times, Bramber was for centuries, a main thoroughfare (something recent traffic-calming measures are designed to stop), with the result that great clouds of dust were sent in all directions by carts and wagons in hot, dry weather, while deep ruts were created in the road when it was wet. The village frequently flooded, which must have made life pretty miserable for the inhabitants. Travellers converged on Bramber from all directions, with trackways leading to the coast, along the tops of the Downs, and into the Weald. Back in 1909, Arthur Beckett was spoilt for choice as to which route to take, but decided to keep heading east -

"... But the hill-tops called, and we climbed to greet them. Wolstonbury called to us from the north, but Ditchling Beacon lay in our way, and our response was given to Ditchling along the top of the Downs. So for some six or seven miles we walked along the summit by the wall of the Weald, past barrows and tumuli and old encampments; past Perching and Fulkling Hils; past Poynings and the Devil's Dyke, until near dusk we came to Pyecombe, tired, hungry and thirsty."

The Normans succeeded in substituting Chichester for Selsey, Arundel for Burpham, and New Shoreham for Old Shoreham, but even William de Broaose, from the commanding heights of his castle was unable to force **Steyning** into a subordinate role. Steyning remained a Saxon town. Even today, looking up and down the High Street, the visitor is aware of the town's solid character. Sturdy timber-framed buildings, surmounted with Horsham-slate still dominate the street. The Chequers and the White Horse look as English inns should look, although both have made concessions to modern tastes in recent years. The grand clock, such a feature of the High Street, came from Michelgrove, the ancestral home of the Shelleys, bought, and then demolished by a vengeful Duke of Norfolk, early in the last century.

Church Street contains Steyning's oldest buildings, including Saxon Cottage, which somehow looks curiously out of place here, with its yellow walls and thatched roof. It is the old Grammer School, founded by Alderman Holland of Chichester in the seventeenth century which is of greatest interest. The building was already three hundred years old when Holland took it for his school. It had originally been in the possession of the Fraternity of the Holy Trinity, in order, which like so many others, was expunged during the Reformation. A glance at the old photograph, which appears on this page, shows a rather different building to the one seen today. Tiles cover the timber work, and these were only removed in fairly recent times, revealing the fine timber-work below. The Grammer School's neighbours, Chatfield House and Holland Cottage are of a similar age.

Ian Nairn was impressed with St. Andrew's, the Parish Church, describing it as, "certainly the best in Sussex, and among the best in the whole country. It was, he said, "virile and inventive", and an exceptional example of Late Norman architecture. This church replaced an earlier Saxon one, founded by St. Cuthman, three hundred years earlier. Cuthman is still well remembered in Steyning, as the Saint who wheeled his old mother her in a wheelbarrow. Locals laughed at their progress, but Cuthman called out to them, "Laugh Man, Weep Heaven!" whereupon the rain fell in torrents. When his cart finally collapsed, Cuthmam made a hut for himself and his mother, and later, despite the taunts of the Devil, built a church. Some people believe that the town grew up as a centre of pilgrimage, for those wishing to pray at the shrine, established in Steyning to the Saint. In the churchyard are several interesting memorials, including

Steyning Church 1903 (FG)

the gravestone of William Cowerson, who led the last of the great smuggling gangs (see p125).

Not far from Steyning is **Chanctonbury Ring**, one of the most prominent points on the South Downs. The name 'Ring' refers to the circular earthwork, which dates back to Iron Age times. The circular clump of beech trees (which were ravaged by the Storm of 1987), were planted by Sir Charles Goring of Wiston House in 1760. A good deal of folklore and superstition is associated with Chanctonbury, and those with an interest to know more should consult Jacqueline Simpson's, *The Folklore of Sussex,* which although out of print is available in most of the county libraries. Hilaire Belloc, although a devout Catholic, was one with a distinctly Pagan hue, as witnessed by the following extract from the 'Four Men,' in which the companions camp for the night in a 'shelter' close to Chanctonbury on Hallowe'en. Gradually all fall asleep in front of a log fire, save one, whose mind could not rest -

"But I was still wakeful, all alone, remembering All-Hallows and what dancing there was in the woods that night, though no man living might hear the music, or see the dancers go. I thought the fire-lit darkness was alive. So I slipped to the door very quietly, covering the latch with my fingers to dumb its noise, and I went out and watched the world. The moon stood over Chanctonbury, so removed and cold in her silver that you might almost have thought her careless of the follies of men; little clouds, her attendants, shone beneath her worshipping, and they presided together over a general silence. Her light caught the edges of the Downs. There was no mist. She was still frosty-clear when I saw her set behind those hills. The stars were more brilliant after her setting, and deep quiet held the valley of the Adur, my little river, slipping at low tide towards the sea."

That was in 1902, before the general advent of motor traffic. Writing in 1936, Belloc bitterly complained that you could, "hear the machine-gun fire of a motor-bicycle on the greensward of Chanctonbury Ring." Something, that to him was little short of scarilege.

Another writer who touched the Spirit of Sussex was Margaret Fairless Barber, better known as **Michael Fairless**. Under this pseudonym, she wrote 'The Roadmender,' a book that was to achieve world-wide popularity. Yet she would never live to enjoy the fruits of success, for she died at Mock Bridge, near Henfield in 1901, aged only thirty-two. She was buried beneath a wooden cross in the churchyard at Ashurst. At the height of her popularity, between the wars, thousands flocked on 'pilgrimages' to both the cottage and the grave. For many years her story was not known. She had taken to writing when struck down by illness. Despite coming from an upper middle class family, she chose to work as a nurse at a clinic in an area of London known as the Jago, where she habitually encountered both violence and drunkenness, as well as disease. She became famous for her compassion, but also for her courage, as she often had to man-handle aggressive patients, or their relatives, out of the clinic. Then, after ten years, came her own illness, and she was forced to abandon her vocation, and seek convalescence in the Sussex countryside.

At first she was able to walk short distances, and chat to the country-folk who passed by her gate, along the Henfield Road. When confined to her bed, she began to write of those conversations. Gradually a series of articles emerged, in which she described the rural world through the eyes of a roadmender. The articles were published in a journal of the day, under the name 'Michael Fairless,' for she wanted no recognition or publicity. After her death, the articles were collated in book form, and appeared as 'The Roadmender,' and were immediately acclaimed in this country. The book achieved its greatest popularity after the First World War, when its message of compassion and hope touched a nerve with all those suffering the bereavement of losing husbands, sons and brothers. It was not until the late 20's that a journalist pieced together the full story of

Margaret Fairless Barber, and her extraordinary life. A life that only increased the public's admiration and respect for her memory, as well as her writings.

Choosing just one extract from that exceptional book is no easy task, but the following description of an old man on his way to the workhouse, and of the widow who intervenes to rescue him from such an indignity, is typical of the style and empathy of Michael Fairless. We find the old man resting by the side of the road, with the roadmender, and a young child with her kitten-

"The old man sat resting: I had promised him a lift with my friend the driver of the flour cart, and he was almost due when the child's grandmother came down the road. When she saw my other visitor she stood amazed.

'What, Richard Hutton, that worked with my old man years ago up at Ditton, whatever are you doin' all these miles from your own place?'

'Is it Eliza Jakes?'

He looked at her dazed, doubtful.

'An' who else should it be? Where's your memory gone, Richard Hunton, and you not such a great age either? Where are you stayin' ?'

Shame overcame in; his lips trembled, his mild blue eyes filled with tears. I told the tale as I had heard it, and Mrs. Jake's indignation was good to see.

'Not keep you on 'alf a crown! Send you to the House! May the Lord forgive them! You wouldn't eat no more than a fair-sized cat, and not long for this world either, that's plain to see. No, Richard Hutton, you don't go to the House while I'm above ground; it'd make my good man turn to think of it. You'll come 'ome with me and the little 'un there. I've my wushin', and a bit put by for a rainy day, and a bed to spare, and the Lord and the parson will see I don't come to want."

She stopped breathless, her defensive motherhood in arms.

The old man said quaveringly, in the pathetic, grudging phrase of the poor, which veils their gratitude while it testifies their independence, 'Maybe I might as well.' He rose with difficulty, picked up his bundle and stick, the small child replaced the kitten in its basket and thrust her hand in her new friend's.

'Then 'oo is grandad tum back,' she said.

Mrs. Jakes had been fumbling in her pocket, and extracted a penny, which she pressed on me.

'It's little enough, mister,' she said.

Then, as I tried to return it: 'Nay, I've enough, and yours is poor paid work.'

I hope I shall always be able to keep that penny; and as I watched the three going down the dusty white road, with the child in the middle, I thanked God for the Brotherhood of the Poor."

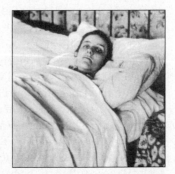

Michael Fairless

THE REFORMATION IN SUSSEX

Henry VIII's break with Rome unleashed forces which were to prove far more potent, and as it turned out, more uncontrollable, than either Henry, or his ministers could have anticipated. Indeed the shadows cast by the religious schism of the 1530's would lead directly to the great storm of Protestant dissent that was to engulf England in civil war over a century later. This century of flux and change was felt with peculiar passion in Sussex, and re-opened the ancient division between east and west, when one part of the county stood for Parliament and the puritan cause, while the other inclined to the King and the established church. Before that was to happen, there would be the greatest re-distribution of land ownership seen in Sussex since the Norman Conquest. There would also be the martyrdom of both men and women, who refused to renounce their religious faith and principles, and whose deaths would affect the cultural atmosphere of the county almost up until our own times.

Late Medieval Sussex

During the last century of the middle ages, Sussex was a county with two histories, a wealden one and a downland one. In the downland and coastal districts of Sussex, the Norman settlement of 1066 remained largely unchanged and unchallenged, but in the wealden areas, particularly in the 'high weald' of eastern Sussex, rebellion and dissent became ever more common. These areas, still considered wild and remote, had not been settled on a large scale until the thirteenth and fourteenth centuries. As the population had increased, so the older manors found it expedient to try and unload some of their surplus population, and what better than to encourage the colonisation of the great wooded areas of the Weald? Colonisation is probably the right word, for these hardy peasants would have needed both strength and fortitude to overcome such a hostile and unpromising environment. This heroic effort, described by historians, Peter Brandon and Brian Short as, "a saga of man against the wild without parallel in medieval England", succeeded because men were prepared to make extraordinary sacrifices in order that they should be their own masters, free of both the squire and the parson.

By the late fourteenth century, the 'open' parishes of the Weald, contrasted markedly with the 'close' parishes found elsewhere in Sussex, where the manor dictated the conditions of daily life and work, and the church captivated men's minds, as well as their souls. In the wealden hamlets, the writ of church and manor counted for little. Here the people survived by their own efforts, and formed their own ideas regarding religion and politics. It is no surprise there-fore to find such communities playing a prominent role in the Peasants' Revolt of 1381, and Jack Cade's equally momentous rebellion of 1450. The distur-bances do not appear however to have travelled further west than Lewes, and made no mark at all upon the social cohesion of such bulwarks of feudal and ecclesiastical power as Arundel and Chichester.

It was also in 1450, that Bishop Moleyns gained the dubious distinction of becoming the only Bishop of Chichester ever to have been assassinated. Fearful of heretics and rebels, Moleyns moved from one mortified manor house to another within his diocese (Amberley Castle being the most obvious example of such a living). With Cade's rebellion at its height, Moleyns attempted to flee the country (he claimed to be going on a pilgrimage), but he was recognised by rebels at Portsmouth and stabbed to death. There was great anger at the power, wealth and corruption of the church, and many people were listening to the heretical preaching of the Lollards, who claimed that the only relationship that mattered was the one between the individual and God. If this were so, then all Abbots, Priors, Bishops, Archbishops and Cardinals were not just an irrelevance, but an abomination in the eyes of God. Such beliefs were not only a danger to the Church, they were a threat to the whole social order. Little wonder then that acts of rebellion were blamed on the Lollards, who risked, if caught, being burned at the stake for heresy.

Amberly Castle in 1903 (FG)

In Sussex the shock troops in the war against the heretics, were the Friars. Once regarded as the friends of the poor and vulnerable, they had by the fifteenth century become overawed with power and wealth, and their earlier vows of poverty had been all but abandoned. In matters of religious zeal however they had lost none of their old resolve, and Friars, acting almost as a religious police, hunted down Lollards across the realm, thereby earning the gratitude of both the Crown and the aristocracy. A minority of Friars broke away from the established orders, and set up on their own, promising to remain true to the beliefs of their founders. Such men gained the trust, and we can say, the love of the common people. No real distinction existed in those days between religion and politics: to challenge the power of the church was equally a challenge to the whole feudal system.

In 1459, Reginald Peacock, the successor to the murdered Moleyns, was himself indicted for heresy. So great was the fear of non-conformity, that even the slightest deviation from religious orthodoxy could lead a man to the stake. Peacock was no Lollard, but in his sermons and in his writings, he had appeared to concur with at least some of their beliefs, even though he had denounced with great vigour their more extreme doctrines. Only by the most grovelling repentance, which included the humiliation of seeing all his scholarly works burned in public, was Peacock himself able to escape the flames. His actual punishment though was severe enough. He was banished to an isolated monastery in the Fens, where he was deprived of all books, save the Bible, and was refused all writing materials. He could discuss no subjects with the monks, except matters of diet and health. So utterly did Peacock disappear from the historical record, that we do not even know when and how he died. Dean Stephens, writing in the last century, thought that Peacock's conceit and arrogance helped bring about his downfall. Stephens wrote -

" His mingled cleverness and excessive vanity made him eager to defend a position in the face of vehement opposition. He loved notoriety, and the more paradoxical and untenable the position he maintained, the better pleased he was, because it afforded more scope for the display of his learning and talent."

Such a description could equally apply to King Henry VIII, or indeed to Thomas Cromwell, the king's evil genius. It is ironic that both the personality and the doctrines of Peacock, so scorned in the fifteenth century, should become the guiding principles of the English state in the sixteenth century. Like Peacock, Henry and Cromwell could not have foreseen the longer term implications of their actions.

Dissolution of the Monasteries

The religious houses in Sussex were both wealthy and influential. Although not as numerous as in other parts of the country, the Sussex monasteries were landowners of considerable magnitude, and none more so than Battle Abbey, often described as the 'seventh rape' of Sussex. Nationally, a third of parishes were granted to the monasteries, in Sussex the figure was 44%. Tithes formed an important part of their income. Great tithe barns were constructed to receive the offerings of the people, some of which still survive to this day, such as the ones at Alciston in East Sussex, and Sullington in West Sussex. When standing inside the massive barn at Alciston, which belonged to Battle Abbey, it is possible to gain some sense of the wealth and power of that institution. Remember also how small the population was at that time compared to today (Even by 1500 the national population was only about three million), and we can begin to realise the resentment that many people must have felt. Instead of working to improve their own condition, they were toiling in order to maintain the great wealth of the Abbey.

Some writers and historians have depicted the dissolution of the monasteries, during the reign of Henry VIII as the abolition of a medieval form of social security. It was G.K. Chesterton who described the monasteries as the "wall of the weak", offering charity and refuge to the dispossessed and feeble. This was indeed the case in certain parts of the country, and particularly in the north, where the people rose up in defence of their monks and friars. It was not so in Sussex. In this county, the monasteries were more concerned with their hunting rights and in staging sumptuous banquets than they were with the alleviation of poverty. Lewes Priory was the most generous of the Sussex orders, spending 3.1% of its yearly income on charitable works, Battle Abbey, despite its extraordinary wealth, was the meanest, donating only 0.6%. Little wonder then that the people of Battle appeared so disinclined to rise up in support of the Abbey, when Thomas Cromwell moved against it in 1538.

It should be remembered Henry VIII had, early on in his reign, been granted the title of 'Defender of the Faith' by the Pope. The King had gained the appreciation of the Papacy for a pamphlet he had written denouncing the views of Luther and the German Protestants. In England the suppression of the Lollards had been so thorough that the nation appeared to be a bastion of Catholic orthodoxy. Yet a careful observer might have anticipated trouble to come, not just in the state of the King's marriage, but also in the condition of his finances. Henry, unlike his cautious and prudent father, wallowed in luxury and revelled in extravagance and show. Descriptions of the King's court, and in particular of the King himself, are breathtaking in their images of ornamentation, ceremony, fine clothes, jewels, trinkets, gleaming diamonds, and shimmering gold cloth. Yet England was no Spain or France, and such opulence was not justified by the economic reality of Henry's England.

Yet there was wealth in England: old wealth and new wealth. The old wealth lay with the monasteries, the new wealth with the rising class of merchants and entrepreneurial farmers. What the new class, and in particular the merchants wanted more than anything was status, and status came through the ownership of land. They had the money to buy, that was not the problem, the difficulty was that the land was not available to be purchased. It was at this point that new voices came to the King's attention, some sincere, others cynical. Dr. Cranmer, who had so impressed Henry with his advice regarding the royal marriage, began to tempt the King with theological criticisms of the monastic system. Thomas Cromwell, a hard-headed clerk in the employ of Cardinal Wolsey, suggested that all Henry's financial problems would be swept aside if the great estates of the monasteries were to become the King's estates, which in turn could be sold to wealthy merchants desperate to acquire landed titles.

What is more, there were precedents. The Pope himself had allowed Henry to dissolve some of the small religious houses. Although this was officially done in the interests of maintaining an efficient and effective monastic system, the Pope would have realised that such measures were really a form of subsidy to the English crown, which given its resolute stand against heresy, was but a small price to pay. Yet precedents are dangerous things, especially when clever advisors gain the ear of a vain King.

The first religious house to be suppressed in Sussex was actually done so with the agreement of the Church in 1525. Bayham Abbey, situated in the heart of the Weald, close to the Kent border, was about as a remote and inaccessible a place as any in the kingdom. Even today, a visitor to the abbey ruins feels a

The ruins of Bayhan Abbey in the early 19th century (WSCC)

sense of isolation. This was no Battle Abbey, but a small order of canons, who not only dispensed charity in the locality, but also provided employment. The eviction of the canons, provoked the fury of the people, who were described by one official as being, "as ungovernable as the terrain." Men with blackened faces, or wearing masks, and armed with swords, longbows, crossbows and clubs, attempted to reinstate the evicted canons. For a week they held the abbey, until they were eventually driven away by force. It was thought that even local landowners, such as George Neville and Alexander Culpeper, sympathised, or even encouraged the rebels. More than anything, this incident demonstrated the independence of spirit of the wealden communities, and their dislike of outside interference in their affairs.

When in 1534, King Henry married Anne Boleyn, having declared himself supreme head of the Church in England, the way was clear for the biggest land grab since 1066.

All in Church and State had to swear an oath of allegiance not just to Henry, but also to Anne. They were also expected to preach in favour of Royal Supremacy over the Church, and against the authority of the Pope. It is perhaps an indication of the nature of human frailty, that most people, be they clerics or clerks, accepted the new order without a murmur. One group who refused to conform were the friars. The very people, so commended for their campaign against the Lollards, now found many formerly heretical ideas being promoted by none other than the King, and his newly appointed Archbishops and Bishops. In the wealden areas of eastern Sussex and Kent, friars took up the cause of a Nun, Elizabeth Barton, who for some four years had been subject to visions. She went into trances and heard voices. She preached with vehemence. Even the Bishop of Rochester believed her to be genuine. None in London paid any attention to her, until she began saying that Anne Boleyn was possessed of demons, and had bewitched the King. Such talk was treason, and the response was swift and merciless. Barton, and several Franciscan Friars were seized, and lodged in the Tower of London. A few days later, without even the pretence of a trial, they were executed. The following year, Dr. Fisher, Bishop of Rochester, followed them to the scaffold.

Over the next four years all the religious houses in Sussex were suppressed, and their estates seized by the Crown. At no time was the pretence dispensed with, that the only reason for the suppression of the monasteries was their corrupt practices. Not that it would have been difficult to find corrupt practices in Sussex. Commissioners, dispatched by Cromwell, reported on the aledged misconduct they discovered. At Boxgrove Priory it was found that the Monks were dirty and unclean, worse still, "they showed a lack of caution in relations with female domestic." They found more time for

Boxgrove Priory (FG)

archery and in playing cards than they did for charitable endeavours. At Lewes, the condemnation could not have been more severe. Cromwell's commissioner, Dr. Layton reported -

"At Lewes I found corruption of both sorts; avowterers [fornicators] and sodomites. And what is worse treason … The suppryor hath confessede to me treason in his preachyng, I have caused him to subscribe his name to the same, submittyng hymself to the kynges mercy and grace. I have made him confesse that the prior knew the sam … And the same suppryor subscribed his name to the said confession against the prior … I then called him "haynose tratur" with the worst words I could deliver, he all the tyme kneeling upon his knees, making intercession unto me, but [I] commaundit hym to appere before you at the Court on Alhalow Day, where you and the kyng should happen to be, and to bring with him his supprior. At my cumming unto you… I shall declare you all at large and the tragedie thereof, so that it shall be in your power to do with hym what you like."

The last phrase sounds very ominous, especially given the fate of Elizabeth Barton and her supporters. The King could not afford to execute too many people however, after all he needed people to work for and run his new Church. Generally speaking, so long as all the allegations were conceded, and guilt accepted, mercy would be forthcoming. Confessions made justifying the policy of suppression so much easier. Many former monks, abbots and canons, were found jobs, often at enhanced rates of pay in the new Church. Others were pensioned off, again at a very handsome rate. John Hammond, the last Abbot of Battle Abbey was given an annual sum of £50 for life, and a fine retirement house in Battle town. Whereas in the north of England, former monks appeared desperate to retain a position which allowed them to follow their spiritual calling, in Sussex, former monks seemed only too pleased to opt for a leisurely life on a handsome pension. No wonder local people shed so few tears at their passing.

Having secured the monastic lands, the King now proceeded to sell off these great estates to the wealthiest men in England. Sir Anthony Brown fared best of all in Sussex, his acquisitions included the 22 manors of Battle Abbey; he had earlier secured the smaller estates of Bayham, Easebourne, and Waverley. Over the following decades, Brown and his descendants increased their wealth, thanks to their new estates. Many hereditary titles followed the land grab - the Browns were created into the Montagues, and played an important role in the life of the country for several centuries to come.

The most notorious of the new landowners in Sussex was Sir John Palmer, a London merchant, who acquired land at Angmering, which had formerly belonged to the Abbess of Fecamp. One of his first actions was drive off the copyhold tenants living on his new land. He ordered that their cottages and orchards should be pulled down, and all the land put over to agriculture. The dispossessed tenants, believing that Palmer had acted illegally, complained to the Star Chamber, but to no avail. In his triumph, Palmer taunted his accusers. "Do ye not know", he told them, "that the King's grace hath put down all houses of monks, friars, and nuns, and therefore, now is the time come when we gentlemen will pull down the houses of such poor knaves as ye be."

Using the latest methods in agriculture, including the sowing of tares to increase the fertility of the soil, Palmer and others like him, secured a wealth from the coastal plain of Sussex that had not been seen since Roman times. Imposing new country houses were built as a result of this wealth, one of the best known being the one built by Palmers's son at Parham. Yet to many such repracious capitalism was an anathema. John Strong, a small freeholding farmer of Poling described Palmer as, "beyng corrupt in conscience, and a man minded muche to averyce."

Counter Reformation and the 'Sussex Martyrs'

Following Henry VIII's death in 1547, he was succeeded by his sickly son, Edward VI. It was during the six year reign of this boy king, that Cranmer was able to push ahead with a genuine reformation of religion, as opposed to the largely financially motivated changes of Henry's reign. Protestant zealots from all over Europe, flocked to England. It was from this time that Protestants from France and the Low Countries began settling in Sussex, with Rye in particular becoming a favourite destination. The introduction of the Book of Common Prayer, and the English translation of the Bible (reading the Bible in English had been one of the main heresies of the Lollards) were the main achievements of Edward's reign. However in the country as a whole, and most certainly in Sussex, the majority of the people remained Catholic in outlook. Many parishes continued with the old form of worship, and may indeed have been largely ignorant of the changes being introduced in London.

Then, in 1553, Edward died, and Mary Tudor, a Catholic, came to the throne. She was the daughter of Katherine of Aragon, and viewed the whole reformation process as not just a heresy, but an affront to both herself and her mother. Mary was initially well received, and there was little popular support for the abortive attempt to place the Protestant Lady Jane Grey on the throne, in her place. Had she lived longer and been more shrewd in her policies, Mary might well have succeeded in sweeping back the Protestant advance. Instead she inflamed the ire of the whole nation by marrying Philip of Spain. To Mary the marriage represented the unity of this country with the most powerful Catholic country in the world, a move that would surely strengthen her hand at home. In the event it has the opposite effect. Protestant propagandists depicted the marriage as a Spanish Catholic takeover of England. It was however the persecution, and then the execution of Protestants that united England against Mary and the Catholic cause.

To the death of famous men, such as Cranmer, Latimer and Ridley, may be added others of more lowly birth, such as those burned at the stake in Sussex between 1555 and 1557. Even today, we still talk of 'Bloody Mary', and have a sense that her reign was characterised by brutal execution on an unprecedented scale. Less than three hundred men and women actually died for their faith during those years. Bad enough, certainly, but in the context of the times hardly outstanding. When thousands of northerners had peacefully marched on London, during the reign of Henry VIII, in the so-called 'Pilgrimage of Grace', calling for a halt to the dissolution of the monasteries, they were met with courtesy. But after they dispersed, Henry had them hunted down, arrested, imprisoned, and executed. The bodies of about 400 'rebels' were hung along the Great North Road. Mary never descended to such arbitrary slaughter, yet it is she who is remembered as the 'bloody' Queen. The reason is simple enough to explain - her counter reformation failed. Protestantism ultimately triumphed, and it was the Protestants who subsequently wrote the nation's history. Many generations of English people were brought up on 'Foxe's Book of Martyrs', which eulogised the Protestant martyrs, and demonised Mary and her Catholic clergy. It was the most widely read book in England after the Bible.

The martyrdoms of Mary's reign also clearly established the idea of 'Catholic Europe'. The belief was that Europe, and Spain and France in particular would stop at nothing to destroy the 'freedoms' of Protestant England. It is ironic then that some of the martyrs were not English at all. Take for instance Deryk Carver, the most famous of the Sussex martyrs. He had been born in Flanders, then under Spanish rule, and fled to England during the previous reign. Carver ran the Black Lion Brewery in Brighton. It was in his premises that prayer meetings were held, and readings made from an English translation of the Bible. At his interrogation, Carver valiantly defended his beliefs, and denounced those of his captors, telling Bishop Bonner that he would not renounce the "true doctrine of Christ". He then told the Bishop that his beliefs were all "poison and sorcery", adding for good measure, "If Christ were here you would put him to a worse death than he was put before." Many of those arrested with Carver and subsequently, displayed similar defiance thereby making their own deaths inevitable.

Richard Hooke of Alfriston stubbornly refused to recant any of his beliefs, nor his condemnation of the Church of Rome. The anger and exasperation of his inquisitors is very apparent from the declaration issued by Bishop Day, which condemned Hooke, and handed him over to the secular authorities for execution -

"Richard Hooke of Alfriston, a child and nursling of devilish iniquity, on account of his manifest wicked errors, detestable heresies, and damnable opinions, opposed, contrary to the Catholic Faith, publicly and pertinaciously defended, has been denounced by us as an obstinate and confirmed heretic. Since Holy Mother Church can do nothing further against such a putrid member, we have handed over to your Royal Highness and the power of your secular arm the said Richard Hooke as a heretic to be punished and broken."

Between 1555 and 1557, ten martyrs, including Carver, were burned at the stake opposite the Star Inn at Lewes (site of the present-day Town Hall). The vaults in which they were imprisoned still survive beneath the Town Hall, and a plaque commemorates those who died, and remained, "FAITHFUL UNTO DEATH". Further executions took place elsewhere in the county. At East Grinstead in 1556, Thomas Dungate, Anne Tree, and John Forman were burned to death in the High Street. A memorial to them is to be found close to the entrance of the parish church. Six men and women from Mayfield were martyred. Other martyrs came from Warlbeton, Heathfield, Rotherfield, Alfriston, Catsfield, Rye, Hellingly and Woodmancote. Only three martyrdoms occurred west of the Adur, that of John Launder at Steyning, and Thomas Iveson and Richard Hook at Chichester. None of these men were natives of the western part of the county, two coming from Godstone in Surrey.

The executions did not have the intended effect. The courageous conduct of the martyrs as the flames were kindled around them only served to convince the onlookers that righteous people were about to die. The executions, carried out in the name of both the Queen and the King, were judged by many as proof of the malignant influence of Spain. The martyrs became national as well as religious icons. In Sussex their legacy was profound, and created a sense of popular Protestantism, that had not previously existed. Throughout the eastern Weald in Sussex, it is still possible to find memorials to the martyrs. There is the obelisk on Cliff Hill at Lewes, and its smaller scale replica in the graveyard of the chapel at Punnetts Town near Heathfield. There is a memorial in the grounds of the United Reformed Church at Mayfield, and one on the south wall of the parish church at West Hoathly. At Warbleton , in the south wall of the churchyard is a memorial to Richard Woodman. Popular Protestantism remained a potent force in Sussex until quite recently. The Orange Order was associated with Bonfire Night parades until early in the twentieth century, and the Sussex Martyrs Commemoration Council was still operating in the county in the 1950's.

Richard Woodman of Warlbleton had been a farmer and ironmaster. He was therefore neither of the peasantry, nor yet from the gentry. He typified many of the Protestant martyrs - people who had improved their station in life by their own efforts. Such industrious and hard working people were increasingly attracted to fundamentalist Protestantism, from which the puritan ideals of later decades would emerge. During the reign of Elizabeth, there was an unprecedented period of industrial expansion in the Weald, often inspired by 'emigre' craftsmen. At Chiddingfold and Ewhurst, Huguenot glassmakers established themselves, while iron masters from the Low Countries, introduced the blast furnace to the wealden iron industry (see p66). Weavers and cloth-makers from overseas added to the growth of trade. Such men not only brought employment into the county, they also brought a resolute Protestant faith with them, which filtered into the native population.

In the low Weald of the west, and in the downland and coastal areas, life and work continued much as it had before. The Sussex gentry, particularly in the west of the county, developed a remarkable solidarity. Such men exercised power as Justices of the Peace, and the Quarter Sessions, held separately in both West Sussex and East Sussex took on the role of a local government. When England was threatened by the Armada in 1588, it was the JP's under the direction of the Lord Buckhurst, the Lord Lieutenant, who organised the defence of the Sussex coast. No other government in Europe would have risked giving so much power to its regions, as the Elizabethan state entrusted to the English counties. Yet such devolution of power, based as it was on the loyalty of the county gentry to the Crown, was not without its potential for conflict.

In 1570 Richard Curteys became Bishop of Chichester. He was a devout, puritan-minded man, and a true believer in the Reformed Faith. He was shocked to discover that many unreformed practices were still carried on in the county. At West Tarring, for instance, the parish possessed both Mass books, and the plate and vestments necessary for saying Mass. Elsewhere he found clergy who were both ignorant and indifferent to the new form of worship. Worst of all, he discovered that the Justices were very lax in taking action against recusants (those who failed to regularly attend divine service). Not only did many of the gentry know of Catholics in the county, and fail to take action, but counted such men as their friends. Prominent Sussex families such as the Howards of Arundel, the Shelleys of Michelgrove, and the Gages of Firle were well known as practising Roman Catholics. Many people in Elizabethan England, including possibly Elizabeth herself, were little concerned with men's religious beliefs, so long as such beliefs did not lead them into treasonable liaisons with foreign Catholic powers. To men like Richard Curteys however, the Pope was the Anti-Christ, and all who followed him were foot soldiers of Satan. To the Sussex gentry, Curteys was viewed with suspicion, and as a disruptive presence in 'their' county.

Curteys however was determined to impose total conformity to the Protestant faith on the people of Sussex. Declaring that preaching was, "the chariot on which salvation rode into the hearts of men", the Bishop determined to face down his powerful opponents, such as Edward Lewkenor of Chichester, and Thomas Palmer of Parham. Such families had done very well out of the dissolution of the monasteries, but were a lot less keen to embrace the fundamentalist Christianity which came in its wake . In an effort to extend his influence across the county, Curteys appointed his brother, Edmund, as vicar of the wealden market town of Cuckfield. Here the tension between Edmund, and the local squire, Henry Bowyer of Cuckfield Place, was even greater than that which existed between his brother and the western gentry.

Matters came to a head, when Edmund accused Bowyer of having made one of his servant girls pregnant, and further alleging that Bowyer's wife had carried out an abortion on the girl. Using his powers, Edmund assembled a coroner's court, with an all female jury, and his wife as the foreman. The verdict of unlawful miscarriage, naming Mrs. Bowyer, scandalised the county. The gentry families of Sussex resolved not just to bring down Edmund, but his brother the Bishop, as well. Bowyer himself, using his powers as a JP, convened his own coroner's court, which declared the miscarriage to have been quite natural, and commended the Bowyers for the compassion they had shown towards this wayward girl. The scandal would not go away, and the matter was raised with Sir Francis Walsingham and the Privy Council.

Walsingham, in order to gauge opinion in the county, wrote to several of the Sussex JP's requesting their view of the matter. The overwhelming response was hostile to the Curteys brothers. Walsingham, convinced by the evidence, denounced Edmund as being the "lewd vicar of Cuckfield", and ordered his ejection from the parish. Richard Curteys remained as Bishop, but was reprimanded in such a way as to undermine his authority. He died a broken man. Some years later, Walsingham learned about the truth of the affair, and was overcome with personal remorse. He saw to it that Edmund Curteys was reinstated in the Church. However Edmund did not return as vicar of Cuckfield, but as vicar of Thorney, an appointment which could hardly have been regarded as being of equal status. As for Bowyer and his allies, no action was taken against them. Men such as these were far too important to be needlessly antagonised.

The arrest of Sir Philip Howard of Arundel and William Shelley of Mitchelgrove for conspiracy and treason took place in the aftermath of the Armada scare of 1588. When the case against Howard for conspiracy collapsed, his accusers fell back on the assertion that Howard had prayed for the success of the Armada, thereby demonstrating his treachery. Shelley was accused of having met with a Papal spy in Patching Copse. His conviction and condemnation was therefore inevitable, and his estates were sequestrated. The intervention of Lord Buckhurst with Lord Chancellor Burghley, proved decisive in ensuring the estates remained in the possession of the Shelley family. Buckhurst persuaded Burghley that William Shelley's cousin, Harry should be granted the sequestrated estates, as he was a man whose religious convictions were beyond doubt. Buckhurst was himself related to the Shelley family, a fact which helps explain his efforts on their behalf. Indeed by the late sixteenth century many of the leading families of Sussex were bound together by ties of kinship as well as those of common interest: however even this would not be sufficient to prevent the county be rent asunder by the violence of civil war in the 1640's.

Mitchelgrove, home of the Shelley's (WSCC)

THE NORTHERN TOWNS – HORSHAM, CRAWLEY & EAST GRINSTEAD

Although still separate towns, Horsham, Crawley and East Grinstead are at risk, at some point in the future, of merging into one large conurbation. Existing planning policies currently prohibit such a development, but with the constant pressure to provide more housing in the south-east of England, it is a brave person who can declare, hand-on-heart, that such policies can be sustained indefinitely.

All three towns have undergone major changes in the last fifty years, and are increasingly taking on the persona of suburban London. Such a change is virtually inevitable given the close proximity of northern Sussex to the capital, yet it is ironic, when one considers the relative remoteness and isolation of these wealden towns, and in particular of East Grinstead until the later eighteenth century. Crawley has changed most of all. It was designated as a 'New Town' after the Second World War, and thousands of Londoners moved into the new estates that were built at that time. Modern Crawley, which is fast approaching a population size of 100,000, has therefore only a tenuous link with its historic past. There is something incongruous, almost bizarre, about the half-timbered buildings including the ancient George Inn, which survive in the High Street surrounded by modern development.

Horsham

Of the three, Horsham has the greatest claim to fame - it was the home of both the Quarter Sessions and the Assizes. It was an ancient borough, and one of the most important market towns in the region. Even in 1903, Lucas still found the old spirit lingering, "Horsham is the capital of West Sussex," he declared, "a busy agricultural town with horse dealers in its streets, a core of old houses, and too many that are new." Only the "venerable homes" in the Causeway still survive intact. Lucas described the street scene, close to the railway station as being, "as fine a mass of timbers, gables, and oblique lines

The Causeway at Horsham in 1903 (FG)

as one could wish, making an effect such as time alone can give. But, he warned, "the days of such relics are numbered." The building of the Westminster Bank in the Carfax in 1897, although modest by modern standards, was thought to be both big and vulgar at the time, and not in keeping with the spirit of the place.

Perhaps the final demise of old Horsham can be dated from the ending of the five hundred-year old weekly market in 1966. Many of Sussex's markets ended in the 1960's, and in Horsham's case it was a crucial turning point. Hilaire Belloc, living at nearby Shipley, was concerned that the old pronunciation of Horsham as 'Hors-ham' had been replaced by the 'meaningless' 'Horsham' by the time he moved into the district in 1906. Belloc thought that local people should be proud of their ancient horse fair, which, he believed gave the town its name. Belloc, went so far as to bribe the guard on the London train to shout out 'Hors-ham' as the train approached Horsham station, with the result that baffled passengers were likely to miss their stop!

Augustus Hare claimed that Horsham owed its name to Horsa, supposedly one of the early Saxon warlords who conquered the land of the Britons (see p18). Horsa was also the name of a Saxon Horse-God, so giving the town the distinction of being named after a deity. However one looks at it, horses seem to have been important to Horsham, so we can sympathise with Belloc's irritation at the change in pronunciation, brought about by the influx of 'furriners' into the town, due largely to the coming of the railway.

In 1449, King Henry VI gave permission to the Archbishop of Canterbury (who held lands in Horsham) to hold a market every Monday in West Street, with the addition of two annual fairs. The area became known as the Archbishopric, later shortened to the Bishopric. The later name survives to this day as a street name, although in the past it designated an entire area. The road today known as the Bishopric was then called Oxford Road. In his reminiscences, published at the end of the nineteenth century, Henry Burstow, bellringer and folk-singer extraordinaire, recalled that in his boyhood the Bishopric was referred to as 'The Rookery.' According to Burstow the name resulted from the belligerent attitude of the local women, who took an insult to one of their number as an insult to all. Burstow recalled how a woman from another part of town, who had a quarrel with a woman in the Bishopric was met by a hostile crowd when she went to confront the woman at her home. She was forced out of the district, but called back at them, "You are a lot of damned old rooks. If you upset one, you upset the lot."

The name 'Oxford Road' may originate with the renaming of the central area of Horsham in the late eighteenth century. Known for centuries as the Scarfolks or Scarfax, this area was once occupied by squatters. These 'scar folk' or poor people later gained rights of tenure, and so the original meaning of the word became forgotten. During the late eighteenth century there was an attempt to standardise English spelling (a process accelerated by the publication of

Dr. Johnson's Dictionary). At Horsham the Scarfax was renamed the Carfax, after the cross-roads of the same name in central Oxford, which are derived from 'carfuks', meaning cross-roads. Although Horsham's Carfax is indeed the central part of the town, where streets come together, it is not a cross-roads. Recently a plaque has been erected at the Carfax, which explains the true origin of the name.

During the later 1960's and 1970's Horsham was altered, almost beyond recognition. Neither developers nor council paid much attention to old streets and old buildings, which were swept away, thus fulfiling the Lucas prophecy. Unsuccessful campaigns were mounted to save some of the older buildings, but with the prospect of new jobs and investment heading Horsham's way, there was little chance of the conservationists being successful. During the 1980's further redevelopment took place. Yet another campaign was launched to save a building, on this occasion St. Mark's Church. Eventually the developers agreed to keep the tower and its spire. And visitors can wonder in incredulity at the nonsense of a neo-gothic church spire surrounded by late twentieth century office blocks.

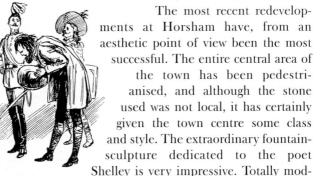

The most recent redevelopments at Horsham have, from an aesthetic point of view been the most successful. The entire central area of the town has been pedestrianised, and although the stone used was not local, it has certainly given the town centre some class and style. The extraordinary fountain-sculpture dedicated to the poet Shelley is very impressive. Totally modern in style, it is appropriate both to the utopian ideas of Shelley himself, and to new Horsham, which is as far away from being a horse-market as one could possible conceive. The only real draw-backs to the new town centre are the intrusive and ungainly CCTV cameras, which this author refuses to see as anything other than an expensive and rather sinister gimmick.

New Year revels at Horsham 1891 (WSCC)

Despite its go-ahead image, modern Horsham does not enjoy Borough status, although it is the home of the District Council, formerly the Urban District Council. The old Borough became defunct in 1834. Its origins were very ancient indeed, dating back to 1290 at least, and probably much earlier still. The official title was, "The Corporation of the Bailiffs and Burgesses of the Borough of Horsham." It once enjoyed power and status, but by the late eighteenth century it had become the play-thing of the Duke of Norfolk. Membership of the Corporation implied no real powers or responsibilities, but merely the opportunity to acclaim the Duke at the annual 'Bailiffs and Constables' Feast.' Food and drink there was a-plenty, with His Grace promising to match any man "bottle for bottle." All came to an end with the election of the Whigs in 1832, who although famous for their 'Great Reform' of Parliament, also reformed local government through the Municipal Corporations Act, which swept away gratuitous and corrupt institutions of which Horsham Corporation was an outstanding example.

Horsham could have applied to become a reformed Borough, but failed to do so, which is hardly surprising given the political corruption then endemic in the town. In the 1870's a campaign was begun to have the town re-incorporated. But Horsham split on political lines, with Liberals in favour and Conservatives against. Without unity the town had no hope of regaining its old status. Benjamin Disraeli, commenting on the dispute, declared that Horsham Borough was "dead and damned." It has certainly showed no sign of being resurrected in recent years.

East Grinstead

For many years East Grinstead was a one-street town, which struggled to survive in the hostile conditions of the High Weald. Its fortunes changed when the Assize Judges, unprepared to make the treacherous journey to Lewes to hear cases, chose East Grinstead as a more convenient destination, and so the town developed around its new judicial status. Some of the oldest and most imposing buildings to survive in the town were built to accommodate the Judges, and are still known as 'Judges Lodgings.' During the reign of Queen Elizabeth I, East Grinstead became the focus of some of the earliest industrial activity in the British isles, with both the glass and iron industries flourishing on its borders. Later came decline: improved communications reinstated Lewes as the judicial

The Judges lodgings in 1903 (FG)

and administrative centre of East Sussex, while the local industries fell into terminal decline. Only the coming of the railway in 1855 revived East Grinstead's fortunes. The wealthy constructed great houses in the surrounding countryside, such as those at Standen, Wakehurst Place, Gravetye, and Borde Hill. To accommodate the growing number of middle class commuters, suburbs began to spread out from the heart of the old town.

Sackville College at East Grinstead certainly has its fair share of history. It was founded in 1609 by the Earl of Dorset, a significant landowner in the district. Far from being a college in the modern sense, its role was that of an almshouse, probably the grandest of its type in the whole county. Even to this day, residence is restricted to elderly folk on low incomes. As recently as the 1930's, the curfew bell was still rung at Sackville College, and the residents still wore the traditional dress: cassocks if male, capes and bonnets if female. Men were always referred to as 'brethren' and women as 'sisters.' A Warden was appointed to look after the spiritual welfare of Sackville's thirty-one residents, as well as to act as administrator.

By far the most controversial of Sackville College's Wardens was the Rev. John Mason Neale, who held the position from 1846, until his death in 1866. Today he is remembered for his hymns (61 of the 473 hymns in the 'Ancient and Modern' are by Neale), but in his own lifetime he was known as one of the most high-profile supporters of the Oxford Movement, whose adherents were later known as Anglo-Catholics. So great were Neale's sympathies for the Roman Catholic form of worship that he was disowned by the Bishop of Chichester, and criticised by the Bishop of London. It was only in 1850 that the Roman Catholic Church was officially allowed to establish a hierarchy in this country, to consecrate churches, and train priests. In the backwoods of Sussex a defiant anti-Catholicism still burned as fiercely as it had done during the days of the Reformation and the Civil war.

In 1851, a 'No Popery' mob attacked Sackville College, their target being Neale himself. In a letter to a friend, Neale described his frightening ordeal -

"The facts are these: That on a certain Tuesday night a mob of about 150 persons, many of them disguised, paraded the town; that they carried torches, firepans, oil, shavings, straw, and other combustibles; that they disturbed the place with their rough music; that they came up to the College, burnt a bier, a pall, and crosses in our field, smashed many of our windows, the stones being thrown with such force as to indent the wall on the opposite side; lighted a fire against our house, which absolutely melted the lead of one of our windows, and the flame of which was seen above the roof - that the mob retired two or three times, and returned to the assault, after having had beer in the town - that when I went out to speak to them they first attack me and afterwards had the cowardice to attack Mrs. Neale; that this took place while my children were known to be seriously ill ..."

Neale was undaunted, and went on to found the Sisters of St. Margaret, an order devoted to tending to the sick and infirm. When, in 1857 one of the Sisters died, Neale attempted to have her buried in her home town of Lewes, again he was attacked by a mob, and was lucky to escape Lewes with his life (see pp92-93) The hatred directed against this quietly-spoken and humble man are a reminder of the deeply Protestant and conservative values of ordinary people in Sussex one hundred and fifty years ago. On the centenary of Neale's death in 1966, the then Archbishop of Canterbury, Dr. Ramsey, preached a sermon at East Grinstead Parish Church, and unveiled a memorial to Neale and his works.

Although there are no longer religious riots at East Grinstead, the town does seem to have a unique capacity for attracting controversial and maverick religions. In and around the town can be found the headquarters, or spiritual homes of the following : Mormons, Jehovah's Witnesses, Countess of Huntingdon's Connexion, New Life Church, Full Gospel Church, Pagan Federation, Baha'i's, Rosicrucians, Opus Dei, Anthroposophical Society, and the Church of Scientology.

It is the last named organisation which has proved the most controversial.

The Scientologists have been at East Grinstead since their founder, the late Ron L. Hubbard purchased Saint Hill House, the former home of an Indian Maharajah, in 1959. At first the local press praised this 'Anglophile' American, who had been a Second World War hero. His ideas of combining religion and psychology seemed original and interesting. However by the late 'sixties, Scientology had become a 'dangerous cult', pilloried in the Press, with allegations of kidnapping and brain-washing. Despite being condemned by governments around the world, the organisation continues to operate successfully from its East Grinstead home.

East Grinstead is justly famous for being the home of plastic surgery, pioneered at East Grinstead Hospital by Archibald (later Sir Archibald) McIndoe. His pioneering work on airmen, shot down during the Second World War, became famous. One of his first patients concluded that he wasn't an airman any more, but just a 'guinea pig of the plastic surgeon.' Although McIndoe's success in rebuilding burnt and mutilated faces silenced his critics, the phrase stuck., and some of his former patients formed the Guinea Pig Club. During the war a pub was opened called the Guinea Pig, which became a popular rendezvous for former patients.

Crawley

Crawley is the cuckoo in the Sussex nest. This New Town, which has developed at a great pace during the last half of the twentieth century, is far more of London than it is of Sussex. The people who came to live here in the 1950's came from the East End. For a time there was some animosity between the locals and the incomers. Sussex people were none too keen on 'furriners', and that was especially true of Londoners. Today there is very little evidence anywhere in Sussex of the old rural, South Country way of life, and even the Sussex dialect has disappeared. We are all in the London mould these days. Yet even so, Crawley still stands apart; its very newness (save the surviving old buildings in the High Street) ensures that.

Crawley is still expanding: the recently built Maidenbower estate has brought thousands more into Crawley, and the growth is set to continue. Many of the town's residents work in 'high-tech' industries, and many more are employed at nearby Gatwick Airport. Gatwick was transformed in the 1960's from being a small rural aerodrome into a major Airport. At the present time (1998) it is still not known whether a second runway will be built at Gatwick, but if it is the effect on this part of Sussex will be immense, and lead almost inevitably to the coalescing of the northern towns mentioned at the beginning of this chapter.

One old Sussex tradition still survives at Crawley. The custom of playing marbles is still carried on at the Greyhound at Tinsley Green. Once just about every pub in the county held a marbles contest at Easter, but now it continues only at the Greyhound, where teams gather from far and wide, often attired in

Worth Church, near Crawley in 1850, showing its Saxon arches (WSCC)

outlandish costumes, to vie for the honour of being the Tinsley Green champions.

Not far from Tinsley Green is County Oak, which today is a housing estate of little interest, but takes its name from a real tree which once stood here. The Oak in question was of great proportions. It was also hollow, and for many years during the eighteenth and early nineteenth people actually lived inside this great tree. It was known as the County Oak because it stood so close to the Sussex/ Surrey border. Oaks were also considered to be very much Sussex trees, indeed so plentiful were they in the county that locals often referred to them as 'Sussex Weed'. The County Oak was finally felled, evidently as a result of a misunderstanding on the part of the lumber-jack, in the early nineteenth century.

Crawley Down, mid-way between Crawley and East Grinstead was, during the early nineteenth century the scene of several 'bare-knuckled' boxing matches, which attracted thousands of spectators of all classes. It was not uncommon for twenty thousand persons to be in attendance, a vast number when the smallness of the local population in those days is taken into account. People came from all over Sussex, Surrey and London to watch these bloody contests. One of the most celebrated took place in 1821, when the two of England's most famous pugilists, Randall and Martin met at Crawley Down. A newspaper of the day described the opening scenes of the contest -

"On Randall stripping every person was astonished at the very fine condition he exhibited. Martin was lighter in person than heretofore, but his condition was good. On placing themselves in their attitudes, Randall was the object of attraction all round the ring, and he stood firm as a rock. The position of Martin was good, but he did not appear to stand as steady as his opponent. A minute elapsed in looking at each other, but the eyes of Randall seemed almost to penetrate into the interior of his opponent. Martin smiled. Randall made a sort of feint with his left hand, which was well stopped by Martin. Randall endeavoured to put in a tremendous right handed blow, but he missed his object. Martin exerted himself to make his right and left tell; but Randall with the utmost dexterity, stopped them both...."

Randall was the eventual winner, leaving Martin in an insensible and bloodied state on the ground. It was half an hour before he regained consciousness. Such extreme and violent outcomes were quite standard for these type of encounters, that took place many years before the Marquis of Queensbury drew up his famous rules, or before boxers were compelled to wear padded gloves.

CENTRAL SUSSEX: CUCKFIELD, LINDFIELD, HAYWARDS HEATH, BURGESS HILL, DITCHLING & HURSTPIERPOINT

Until the coming of the railway in the 1840's, the central part of Sussex was very sparsely populated, with the small towns of Cuckfield and Lindfield being the major centres of population. The district was not considered good farming land, and was therefore somewhat neglected by the great landowners of Sussex. The railway changed everything, it gave rise to the new towns of Burgess Hill and Haywards Heath, sometimes referred to as the 'mushroom towns', because they grew up 'overnight.' There is therefore a marked contrast between the old and historic settlements of Mid Sussex, and the Victorian towns which displaced them.

Haywards Heath cannot boast a long or ancient history. Muster Green on the A272, to the west of the town is perhaps its most historic area. It was on this green, in the heart of the county, that the members of the Sussex militia would assemble. The buildings facing the Green today date from the Victorian period. Indeed prior to the railway coming here in 1841, Haywards Heath was just barren heathland, with a small and transitory population.

Haywards Heath displaced both Lindfield and Cuckfield, two large villages with much of historic interest. At Cuckfield a visitor will find many old buildings, including the old inn, the Talbot, used for sittings of the local magistrates until 1888. The old seventeenth century school is found close to the church. Cuckfield church has a noble shingled spire, and a traditional Horsham stone roof. The vaults are open to public inspection. Lindfield today is a centre of retired affluence, and its historic buildings have been restored to a high standard. The Tiger inn is now a private residence. The village once had several 'cottage industries', producing goods as varied as paper, gloves, candles and pianos. Before the railway, the coaching road from London passed through the village.

Burgess Hill was little more than a farm prior to 1841, and it too owes its existence to the railway. The enclosure of common land around Burgess Hill allowed the new town to expand, and soon its population quickly exceeded that of its older neighbours, Ditchling and Hurstpierpoint.

Central Sussex Before the Railway

Poverty was rife in Mid Sussex before the railway came to transform the fortunes of the district. Following the Norman Conquest, much of the land here was granted to William de Warrene. William and his wife, Gundrada, were civilised and pious people by the standards of their own times. They had numerous churches built, and once attempted to make a pilgrimage to Rome.

Yet by our standards they were unyielding masters. Much of the land was set aside for hunting, either in the form of Royal forests, or aristocratic 'chases'. As a result many poor people resorted to poaching.

In 1218 Thomas de Dene was charged at the King's Bench with assaulting a number of gamekeepers at Cuckfield, employed by Earl de Warrene. A mob armed with bows and arrows had swarmed across the estate, and fought a battle with the keepers, one of whom, William de Legh later died of his injuries. In 1379, a gang of forty-two poachers, one of whom was an ordained priest, were engaged in poaching at Ditchling and Cuckfield. The Peasants' Revolt of 1381 gained much support from this part of Sussex, as did Jack Cade's rebellion of 1450 (see p45). One of Cade's lieutenants was Gilbert Homewoode of Cuckfield, who was later pardoned by King Henry VI for his part in the uprising.

Skirmish between Poachers & Keepers

Smuggling (see pp118-126) was rife in the district during the eighteenth century. It was believed that a property known as 'Harradines' in Little London Lane at Cuckfield was used as a regular depot for smuggled goods. It is even said that the local JP, Sir Peter Cherry had taken bribes from the smugglers to turn a blind eye to their activities. It is believed that the last major consignment of contraband, on this occasion tobacco, passed through Cuckfield in 1855.

Iron smelting and lime burning

The rise of the Sussex iron industry during Tudor times brought employment into the district, and made local families who ran the industry, such as the Challoners, the Bowyers and the Burrells very rich. Two hundred years ago, a book entitled, 'Account of the Preparing and Refining of such Metals as are got in England', by J. Ray, draws on the knowledge of Walter Burrell of Cuckfield to explain the iron smelting process in the Sussex Weald. The ironmasters used different combinations of ore, or 'mine' as he calls it, in order to get the right blend. After being smelted, it was then fired again in order to remove impurities. Molten metal flowed into a large hollow, known as a sow. Smaller moulds were known as pigs. Each pig weighed about one thousand pounds. It took six days to prepare the hearth and furnace, and the last day, on which the iron was made was known as Founday. It was reckoned that one stone hearth, on which the iron ran, would last about forty Foundays before it would have to be replaced. At no time would the fire be allowed to go out.

Pieces of sows and pigs would then be broken off, reheated, and then beaten into manageable sheets of iron, as Ray's account explains -

"The Sow, at first they roll into the Fire and melt off a piece about three-fourths of a hundredweight, which so soon as it is broken off they call a Loop. This Loop they take out with their Shingling Tongs and beat it with Iron Sledges upon an Iron Plate near the Fire, that it may not fall in pieces, but in a capacity to be carried to the Hammer. Under which they, then removing it and drawing a little water, beat it with the Hammer very gently, which forces cinder and dross out of the matter: afterwards by degrees, drawing more water, they beat it thicker and stronger till they bring it to a Bloom, which is a four square mass of about two feet long. This operation they call Shingling the Loop."

The local industry was unable to complete with the more efficient and productive processes introduced into the north of England following the Industrial Revolution in the second half of the eighteenth century. The last Sussex furnace, at Ashburnham was finally put out in 1812. Only the old hammer ponds and overgrown sows survive as a reminder of what was once a thriving industry.

Also to be found in the wealden landscape are the remains of old marl pits and lime kilns. The poor quality of the soils in this part of Sussex, led to farmers adding marl to their fields, in the belief that this increased soil fertility. Marl pits of considerable size were located at Borde Hill, Hatchgate, Horsgate, and Lucastes. During the seventeenth century lime replaced marl as a more effective fertiliser. Lime was made from chalk quarried in the South Downs, and fired in local kilns. Tell-tale plumes of smoke, drifting across the country-side, would have identified the numerous lime kilns that operated between Borde Hill and Haywards Heath. A description of the process comes from Arthur Young -

"The process in the burning is to lay at the bottom of the kilns a little faggot wood, and on that a small quantity of cordwood, covered with some straw; upon this is laid coal, and on the coal chalk; this is continued until the kiln is three quarters full, when the faggots are lighted. After this the kiln is in constant burning the whole season, whatever quantity of lime is drawn from the bottom, the same quantity of chalk and coal is thrown in, the kiln always being full."

The coal was brought by sea from Northumberland and Durham. For every three tons of chalk fired, about one ton of lime would be produced. Depending on the quality of the soils, lime would be added to the land every third, fourth, or fifth year.

The Railway and Enclosure

As early as 1823, a horse-drawn railway between London and Brighton had been proposed, but never amounted to anything. It was in July 1837 that the Royal assent was finally given to the construction of a steam railway from London to Brighton. Work began the following spring, and was completed by the summer of 1841 - a remarkable achievement. The construction of the railway involved the digging of deep cuttings, as well as the construction of a viaduct, and a tunnel through the Downs. The small rural population of the district was swelled by an influx of navvies, over 6,000 at the height of the construction work. The census of 1841 showed that in many Mid-Sussex villages and hamlets the navvies outnumbered the local population by a considerable degree.

The pay and conditions of these first railway workers were very poor. One man was burnt to death inside his wooden cabin, when a fire he lit to warm himself engulfed the straw bed he was sleeping on. Another young worker, aged only sixteen was crushed by the wheels of a cart. Such deaths were regarded as almost routine, and therefore created no special concern.

Sussex, the old, inaccessible county, cut off from London by the Weald, was being dramatically transformed. One contemporary observer wrote that, "as soon as daylight peeps out the whole neighbourhood is alive." Several farms were cut in two by the railway. Two cottages, owned by farmer Molineux of Boltro Farm had to be demolished. Henry Upton at Great Haywards Farm must have watched with incredulity as first the railway, and then the new town of Haywards Heath altered forever the view he and his forebears had known for centuries.

The enclosure of common land, and its subsequent sale to private owners between 1828 and 1855 had a profound impact, and enabled developers, particularly at Burgess Hill, to begin the process of urbanisation.

Keymer Common was the first area enclosed. This took place in the decade before the railway was built, and as a result sale prices were relatively low. The most favourable land was sold, the remainder was distributed amongst the various tenants and copyholders of the Manor of Keymer. Enclosure obliged the new owners to literally enclose, either by fencing, hedging or ditching, their new land. For some the cost of this was too great, and they quickly sold their allocation. One former tenant sold his plot to a army officer for £5, who, when the demand for houses increased, following the arrival of the railway, was able to sell the clay on his land for brick-making. Land prices increased seven or eightfold in fifty years.

Clayton Common was enclosed in 1855, following an auction at the Friar's Oak Inn at Clayton. Plots facing the recently laid-out roads fetched up to £78 per half-acre, others considered to be less commercially attractive went for about half that amount. So great was the amount of money raised, that the sale produced a profit, which was then distributed amongst the former tenants, who received this money on top of their land allocation.

By the end of the nineteenth century suburban streets sprawled out into the rural areas. At Haywards Heath, the Sergisons of Cuckfield Place had sold off great parts of their estate to the developers, who lost no time in erecting hundreds of new houses. This dramatic change to the landscape did not meet with universal approval, writing in 1894, Augustus Hare commenting on Haywards Heath wrote - "Here, till recently, was a wild heath with fine groups of fir trees. The land has been cut up and sold in small portions by the Sergisons, and is now a colony of cockney villas, and the roads both to Lindfield and Cuckfield are lined with lamps."

Cuckfield Place

Cuckfield Place was built by the ironmaster, Henry Bowyer in 1574. His conflict with the local puritan vicar created a great scandal (see p55) The Bowyers were not noted for their forgiving nature. This vengeful legacy was momentarily abrogated during the next century, when Lady Dorothy Bowyer married Sir John Shurley. The couple demonstrated both piety and generosity, and Lady Dorothy was mourned by local people when she died in 1640. The epitaph on her tomb reads - "She was a merite beyond most of her time for her purse was open to a prophet's name; her pitty was the clothing of the poore; her piety the Mother of her practise; her devotions were daily offerings to God; her mercy sure against condemnation and all her minutes were steppes to Heaven."

Such sentiments could not be used to describe the Sergison family who lived at Cuckfield Place during the eighteenth and nineteenth centuries. The family adhered to some strange practices, including the burying of deceased members of the family by torchlight, in the middle of the night. On succeeding to the estate in 1811, Colonel Francis Sergison is supposed to have stood up in his carriage as he approached Cuckfield, shouting out wildly, "It's Mine! All Mine!" Not for long however, for a year later he was dead. His sister, Ann, now set out to disinherit her brother's daughter, claiming that she was actually the illegitimate daughter of a Dublin bar-maid, whom her brother's wife, unable to have children herself, had purchased for seven shillings and sixpence. The scandal led to the courts, where Ann Sergison successfully proved her case.

Ann showed no humanity to the widow and the girl, both of whom she summarily evicted. She lived at Cuckfield Place with her timorous husband, the Rev. Pritchard. The couple adopted the name, Pritchard-Sergison. Ann outlived her husband by many years. She was known for her vindictiveness and cruelty. Many local people believed her to by a witch, and she was known as 'Wicked Dame Sergison'. After her death in 1848, people claimed to see her ghost, swinging on the gates of Cuckfield Place, and carters would not take their wagons down the adjacent road after dark. There is a story of how three local vicars got together to exorcise her spirit, which they supposedly 'drowned' in the font of Cuckfield Church.

Ann's son inherited his mother's temperament, and was considered the rudest man in the district. Although Ann had lived to be 85, few of her descendants reached 40. the family line died out in 1912, when, following a Ball, Charles Warden Sergison caught a 'cold' which apparently caused his death. His wife also died shortly afterwards. Some years earlier the house was nearly destroyed in a fire. Harrison Ainsworth based his novel, 'Rookwood' on the true life happenings at Cuckfield Place.

Danny

Like Cuckfield Place, Danny, near Hurstpierpoint, is an imposing Elizabethan mansion, and one of the last of its type built in the country. For nearly three hundred years, up until 1980, the estate was in the ownership of the Campion family.

The earliest reference to Danny comes from 1343, when John de Warrene, granted a license to Simon de Pierpoint to enclose the 'wood at Daneghithe.' It

was the Pierpoints who built the first manor house at Danny. Their tenure was not a happy one. It is said that Simon de Pierpoint was an oppressive tyrant, who murdered several of his tenants. They in turn rose up against him, setting fire to and destroying the manor house.

Danny during the Regency period (WSCC)

The Pierpoints fled, and the estate ultimately passed to the Dacre family, and it was they who built the present-day house, sometime between 1582 and 1595. During the troubled years of the seventeenth century (see p77), the Dacre family are to be found on opposing sides in the Civil War. George Dacre, created Baron Goring in 1628, was a prominent Royalist. Before the war he had helped arrange the marriage of King Charles to Henrietta Maria of France. During the war he was created Earl of Norwich and commanded the Royalist forces in Kent and Essex. George's sister, Anne, had married Sir Anthony Stapley, a Member of Parliament, who along with Oliver Cromwell and others, signed the death warrant of Charles I in January 1649.

In 1652 Danny was sold to Peter Courthorpe, whose only daughter married Henry Campion of Kent. During the early eighteenth century, the Campions substantially altered and extended Danny, adding a grand, classical facade.

In 1918, the members of the Imperial War Cabinet, including Lloyd George and Winston Churchill, met in secret at Danny to hammer out the terms of the Armistice, which was to bring an end to the First World War. After the Second World War the house was turned into a private school. The estate however remained in the ownership of the Campion family until 1980, when the then heir, James Campion let it be known that he did not wish to be a country gentleman, but instead chose to work with the poor in India. Proceeds from the sale of the estate paid the costs of building a medical centre in Madras.

Wing's Place, Ditchling

Wing's Place at Ditchling, variously known as Anne of Cleves House, the Old House and the Ancient House, is one of the best surviving Tudor buildings in Sussex. Despite local legend, Anne of Cleves, Henry VIII's fourth wife never lived here, although she was granted the house and adjoining lands by the King, not as a wedding gift, but as a means of buying her off after the marriage was dissolved.

The King had been persuaded by Thomas Cromwell to marry Anne for political reasons. She was a Protestant Princess, and an alliance between Cleves, then an independent German statelet, and England was very desirable. Henry, still grieving from the loss of Jane Seymour, who had died in childbirth, agreed to the match after being shown a portrait of Anne, which

Ditchling Old House 1903 (FG)

showed her to be an attractive woman. However the reality did not match the image. On their first meeting, Henry recoiled from Anne, who he found to be plain, even ugly. The marriage was never consummated, and was therefore easy to annul. In order to placate Anne and her kinsmen, Henry bestowed titles and lands upon her, including the Manor of Ditchling.

Anne lived happily at Richmond, outliving Henry by eleven years. At the end of her life, during Mary's reign she is supposed to have converted to Catholicism. Thomas Cromwell, the architect of the whole fiasco did not fare so well. Shortly after the annulment he was arrested, charged with treason and beheaded.

The Cat House, Henfield

Of all the old houses and buildings at Henfield, none attracts more interest and comment than the Cat House. Decorated all around its walls with images of cats and birds, it is a cause of considerable curiosity to visitors.

The house itself is timber-framed, and of considerable age. Its famous illustrations are more recent, and date back to a famous dispute that arose in the middle of the nineteenth century between a local builder, Bob Ward, and the founder of the Lancing College, the Rev. Nathaniel Woodard. Ward had a pet canary, Woodard a cat. One fateful day Woodard's cat killed Ward's canary. Ward's fury knew no bounds. He went so far as to decorate the outside of his house with images of the cat and the canary - a constant reminder of the atrocity. Along the eaves of the house, Ward placed bunches of scallop shells on wires, which he pulled vigorously whenever Woodard passed by on his horse. There was even a mechanically operated black figure that would emerge menacingly from an alcove at the end of the house (locals dubbed it the 'Zulu Hole').

The torment only ended with Ward's death. However the new owner retained the images of the cats and birds, as have all subsequent owners, and the house has ever since been known as the Cat House.

As well as Lancing, there are also Woodard schools at Hurstpierpoint and Ardingly. Woodard mission, back in 1848 was to "educate the Middle Classes", who had recently been enfranchised by the Great Reform Act. **Ardingly** is today principally associated with the South of England Show, held near the village every June. Nearby is Wakehurst Place, with its much visited gardens. This was once the home of the Culpeper family. During the Civil War (see p85), Sir John Culpeper steered a difficult middle course between the Royalist and Parliamentary interests. In 1648 he represented a group of Sussex gentry at Westminster, who had complaints concerning the conduct and alleged excesses of the Grand Committee at Lewes.

North Common at **Chailey** is said to mark the exact centre of the county of Sussex. From the common, impressive views of the surrounding countryside can be enjoyed, taking in Firle Beacon, Mount Caburn, Ditchling Beacon, and even as far as Bignor Hill in the west. Chailey lies on the thick gault clay, used in the last century to make building bricks and pottery. Ades, the old red brick manor house still stands at Chailey, as does the windmill, blown down in a storm in 1929, but subsequently restored.

Plumpton is another old wealden village, its name literally means 'plum farm'. At one time it was possible to see the great cross cut in the turf on the Downs here, following Simon de Montfort's victory over Henry III at the Battle of Lewes in 1264. There is a large V-shaped group of firs at Plumpton Place, planted in 1887 to commemorate Queen Victoria's Golden Jubilee. The Sun Inn boasted Sussex's most loyal customer. In 1975, eighty-one year old

Frank Higgins was presented with a pewter tankard for his continuous custom at the Sun since 1925. For several years afterwards, at each subsequent 'anniversary', the landlord would mark the occasion by opening a bottle of 100-year-old-scotch.

Newick is a pleasant East Sussex village with a village green, a row of old and interesting houses and cottages, and a well preserved church with a sandstone tower. Of most interest is the Bull Inn, which is not named after the animal of that name, but after the 'Papal Bull', for Newick was once on the Pilgrims' route to Canterbury. Sussex, and its pubs in particular abound with ghost stories. Surely the most bizarre haunting in Sussex concerns the Bull Inn at Newick. According to the Evening Argus in 1967, one of the bars was haunted by a large 'ball', which would appear from nowhere, roll across the floor, and then simply vanish.

THE CIVIL WAR IN SUSSEX

The English Civil War began in the autumn of 1642, and rumbled on intermittently until the Royalist cause was finally crushed at the Battle of Boscobel in 1651. However to all intents and purposes the Royalists were a spent force after their crushing defeat by the New Model Army at the Battle of Naseby in the summer of 1645. As far as Sussex is concerned, the fighting was of an even shorter duration, beginning with the Royalist seizure of Chichester in November 1642, and ending with the fall of Arundel Castle to Parliamentary forces in January 1644. The following year though saw the abortive rising of the Clubmen. Discontent in the county continued until the military garrisons were withdrawn in 1648. Finally in 1651, the fugitive Prince Charles sailed from Shoreham, to a life of exile for nine years in France. Sussex was deeply divided by the war; and the growing differences between the east and west of the county, in matters of both politics and religion were heightened. The powerful county government, developed by the gentry during Elizabeth's reign, was shattered and would never be fully recovered.

Nationally, the war was a conflict between Parliament and the Crown, in which each attempted to assert its rights and privileges. In Sussex, the county divided along historic lines, with the east of the county being solidly for Parliament, while the west tended to support the King. For the Royalists, Sussex represented the gateway to London from the south. If London fell, the war would be over. For the same reason, Parliament realised that Sussex had to be made safe against a Royalist incursion. In the autumn of 1642, Pym and Hampden, the Parliamentary leaders, had good reason to depend on the loyalty of Sussex, although as we shall see this confidence was not always well founded.

East Sussex was staunch in its support for Parliament. But in many respects this unity of purpose was a fragile one, for it included within its ranks both moderates and puritan zealots. The spread of Puritanism in the wealden areas has already been discussed, and its influence increased throughout the first half of the seventeenth century. Jury lists and baptismal records for this period reveal a large number of puritan Christian names - names which reveal the extreme piety and commitment of these people to their beliefs. Some of the more extreme examples include - Faint-not Kennarde, of Chiddingly; Stand-fast-on-High Stringer, of Crowhurst; The-peace-of-God Knight, of Burwash; Fight-the-good-fight-of-faith White, of Ewhurst; Be-courteous Cole of Pevensey; Safety-on-High Snat of Uckfield; Search-the-Scriptures Moreton, of Salehurst, and the not to be forgotten, Fly-fornication Richardson, of Waldron. Such persons do not flinch from the thought of war, on the contrary they rejoice in the opportunity it affords to smite the forces of darkness. Such names were largely confined to the east of the county, and rarely occurred in the towns and villages to the west of the Adur.

Just prior to the outbreak of the Civil War, a bloody uprising against English rule took place in Ireland, during which many English and Anglo-Irish Protestants were massacred. A national fund was established, in order to relieve the distress of the survivors. It is noticeable that the parishes in the west of the Sussex contributed less than those in the east and some made no contribution at all. At Burwash the people raised the handsome figure of £39, an amount surpassed by the inhabitants of Mayfield, who contributed £45 to the fund. These were large sums of money for the times. As early as 1634, the spread of Puritanism in the eastern rapes of Sussex was causing concern. In that year Archbishop Laud reported to the King that "the bishop of Chichester certifies all well in his diocese save only in the east part, which is far from him, he finds some Puritan Justices of the Peace have awed some of the clergy into like opinion with themselves."

In Rye in particular, the established clergy had been displaced by fundamentalist preachers, who themselves were regarded as insufficiently robust by the most extreme puritans, represented by the likes of Samuel Jeake and John Coulton. These earnest

The causeway to Rye (Cambar Castle in the distance (WSCC)

young men frequently lambasted the vicar for allowing the 'ungodly' to be buried within the grounds of the church, and for offering up prayers to the same. Jeake, who was only nineteen when the war commenced, came from a staunchly puritan family, and was, even at this early age, an able and articulate public speaker and pamphleteer.

In religious terms, the supporters of Parliament divided into two groups, the more pragmatic Presbyterians, and the more fundamentalist Independents. In East Sussex, the moderates were represented by Sir Thomas Pelham of Lewes, the senior Justice of the Peace in the east, who enjoyed the confidence of most of his fellow magistrates. Pelham saw the war in terms of political objectives, rather than believing himself to be part of a great crusade against Popery. His own view was that the war should be regarded as "….a demonstration against the King which would persuade him to govern with greater respect for the desires of men of property." It had been the King's imposition of taxation, without recourse to Parliament, that had so inflamed men like Pelham.

A minority of the East Sussex gentry and clergy remained loyal to the

Crown. The Gage family of Firle were well-known Catholics, and therefore hardly likely to be found siding with puritans. The Lunsfords of East Hoathly were bitter rivals of the Pelhams, and had scandalised the local gentry, when one of their number, Thomas Lunsford, had attempted to murder Sir Thomas Pelham. When the King appointed Lunsford to high office in 1641, the House of Commons denounced the move, describing Lunsford as "a man of decayed and desperate fortune, most notorious for outrages". As for the clergy, Richard Goffe, vicar of East Grinstead told his parishioners that he, "cared not a figg for the parliament". The Rev. Thomas Sharpe of Beckley, found himself in a minority of one at a public meeting in Battle, when he spoke in favour of Church and King, "They gayned me the repute of the greatest anti-parliament man in these parts," he later complained. Yet these dissenting voices were few and far between, most people in the east of the county were happy to take their lead from Sir Thomas Pelham. Interestingly, Battle, an apparent bastion of Protestantism in the 1640's, had in Elizabeth's time been described as, "the most popish town in all Sussex." The growing tendency to associate patriotic endeavour with Protestant zeal helps to explain the shift of religious affiliation at this time, which ultimately gave rise to the notion of the English being God's new 'chosen people'.

In the west of Sussex the picture was far more confused. On the face of it, the King should have been able to count on widespread support from the local aristocracy and gentry. Thomas Howard, Duke of Norfolk, was after all a Catholic, as was his neighbour, Sir John Shelley of Michelgrove. The Howards were not the force they had once been however, and recent elections had broken their domination of the parliamentary representation in the west. Sir John Shelley was old and infirm, and hardly able to rally the King's interests. Viscount Montagu at Cowdray was also a Catholic. His influence can be seen in the large number of burgesses at Midhurst who refused to sign the oath of loyalty to Parliament. As for the clergy, there loyalty was not in doubt, influenced as they were by the Arminian practices of the Bishop of Chichester. The attitude of the clergy was aptly summed up by one country parson who declared, "Whatsoever the King commands, we are all bound to obey, whether it be good or evil."

Yet at Petworth, the Earl of Northumberland supported Parliament. More importantly, in the county town and cathedral city of Chichester, the burgesses were largely in support of Parliament, including William Cawley, one of the city's two Members of Parliament, and Alderman Henry Chitty, the captain of the trained band of Chichester. The trained bands had been established during the early years of James I reign, when an invasion of England still seemed a distinct possibility. Each county had a trained band, with an appointed captain, who had the key to the county magazine, and was therefore, in the context of the civil war, a key player. At Lewes the trained bands were captained by Herbert Morley, a devout puritan, who also enjoyed the confidence of Sir

Thomas Pelham. For both sides, the position of Portsmouth, and its governor, George Goring was of great strategic significance. Goring had assured Parliament of his support, and accepted money for re-fortifying the town. What Parliament did not know at that stage was that Goring had received similar payments from the King, in return for his promise of loyalty.

The First Campaign

On 7 November 1642, the King issued a proclamation, in which he offered his "grace, favour and pardon to his inhabitants of his County of Sussex, with the exception of Herbert Morley, Esq., and Henry Chittey, citizen of Chichester." At the time this proclamation was issued, the Royalists in and around Chichester had already hatched a plot to seize the city and then the entire county for the King. The two main players in this conspiracy were Sir John Morley (no relation to Herbert Morley) of West Dean, who also had a house within the cathedral close, and Edward Ford of Uppark, who had recently been appointed as High Sheriff of Sussex by the King. Morley was a Member of Parliament, and could count on the support of four other West Sussex MP's: Christopher Lewkenor (Chichester), Sir Thomas Bowyer (Bramber), Thomas Leeds (Steyning), and Thomas May (Midhurst). Significantly the twelve remaining members in the western rapes remained loyal to Parliament, or at the very least were unprepared to commit themselves to the cause of the High Sheriff.

To begin with at least, everything went well for the west Sussex Royalists. Ford used his position as High Sheriff to call out the county militia. The militia was largely made up of labourers and servants from the great country estates, whose masters understood the militia to be a form of collective defence in the event of invasion. When Ford raised the militia in November 1642, it was generally assumed that his intention was to safeguard the borders of the county, and it was on this basis that most of the gentlemen of the western rapes responded. Ford had other plans though, and marched his force of nearly a thousand men on Chichester. Within the city itself, men loyal to Sir John Morley seized the armoury, and then opened the city gates, to allow Ford's men to enter. This act of "treachery" took the Parliamentary party within the city wholly by surprise, and Henry Chitty, William Cawley and other parliamentarians were forced to flee Chichester, without either money, clothes or provisions.

Having triumphed, the Royalist cause now failed to build on its success. The first blow came almost immediately, with news that Portsmouth had fallen to the parliamentarians. The Navy had declared for Parliament, a turn of events that caused George Goring to cut his losses and run. The late governor had of course promised support at various times to both sides, and was later accused of having spent the money given him by both King and Parliament to defend the city on gambling. It was to Portsmouth that Chitty, Cawley and co. now sought refuge.

Back in Chichester, Edward Ford, as impetuous as ever planned to secure Arundel Castle, and then to capture Lewes. The first aim was easily achieved, the second proved more elusive. Supported by Sir Edward Bishop and the Earl of Thanet, Ford came over the Downs, and occupied Steyning. It was here that his men ransacked the local shops. News of such behaviour infuriated many of the western gentry who had contributed men to the militia. Sir John Chapman felt so strongly that he sent word that his men should return home at once. Ford regarded this as desertion, and sent a party of armed cavaliers to seize the horses in Sir John's stables as a reprisal. Sir John Chapman was not alone amongst the western gentry in feeling that the High Sheriff had betrayed their trust. What the incident proved was that the aspiration of dignified neutrality was a forlorn hope in the context of a civil war.

The Royalist forces massed at Henfield, where Henry Bishop, the brother of Edward Bishop was the major landowner. From here they intended to attack Lewes from the north, coming across Haywards Heath (which in those days was just a heath, devoid of population). On paper the omens were not good for Lewes. There were no parliamentary forces in the area, save for Herbert Morley's trained band. For Morley and his men however the time had come, and although greatly outnumbered, and we can assume outgunned as well, the Lewes men with God's cause before them, marched out to meet their enemy. They fought for over an hour with "great fierceness", and utterly routed the Royalists. On surveying the debacle, it was said that Ford "conveyed himself away and left his men in the lurch to shift for themselves." From the puritan parishes of the eastern Weald, men came forward, offering their services to Morley, who now laid plans for a counter-attack.

In London Parliament had ordered Sir William Waller, one of their most accomplished generals, to make haste for Sussex. Herbert Morley was granted the rank of Colonel, and led his men across the Adur. Arundel Castle fell , when "thirty-six daring spirits" surprised the garrison, exploded a 'petard' at the castle gate, and charged in with drawn swords. Amongst those taken prisoner were Sir Richard Lechford and his son, a "great Papist", and Captain Goulding. Also taken were 100 horses, as well as weaponry and provisions. On 20 December, the forces of Colonel Morley and Sir William Waller converged on Chichester.

Waller positioned his canon on the Broyle, north of the city, and periodically fired over the city walls, causing consternation within the ranks of the besieged garrison. Fearing that Waller's men might attempt to enter the city via the suburb of St. Pancras, which was built-up against the walls, Royalist soldiers forced out the inhabitants and then set fire to their dwellings. Most of the inhabitants were needle-makers, who lost more than their homes as a result of this raid. Not surprisingly, many now offered their services to Waller and Morley. The Royalists were simply playing for time, and with no realistic expectation of being relieved they were forced to surrender. Waller entered the city in triumph. Some of his men, led by Sir Arthur Hasilrige (described by Clarendon as "that absurd bold man") plundered the cathedral and chapter house, destroying "idolatrous images", and searching for hidden gold and silver vestments. Hasilrige's men banged and knocked at panels and screens, listening for any indication that would suggest concealment, and at last Sir Arthur was observed to break into a spirited jig, shouting out, "Hark boys! It rattles! It rattles!" They had found their treasure.

An attempt to assassinate Waller, by igniting barrels of gunpowder stored in the basement of his quarters in the city, was discovered. To the puritan soldiers the discovery of this plot, together with their military success was all due to God's providence. Even the rains had held off until the siege had ended. With Sussex safe once more for the parliamentary cause, Waller withdrew, leaving the county in the hands of Colonel Morley and the reinstated Cawley and Chitty. The Speaker of the House of Commons wrote to Cawley, instructing him how best to provide for the future defence of the county -

"You shall take away the arms and horses of such as do refuse to contribute horsemen or arms ... and you shall force all Papists, and persons disaffected to the Parliament, to contribute towards the maintenance of your army."

Many expected the Royalists to attempt another campaign in Sussex, but as the spring and then the summer of 1643 came and went without incident, it seemed perhaps the danger had passed. The ever vigilant Colonel Morley was less sanguine, being ever suspicious of the neutrality cherished by the gentry of the western rapes, and the danger posed by Ralph Hopton, the Royalist general, who had gained great victories in the west of England. "This approaching cloud", Morley wrote, "may raise a storm in Sussex, which county is full of neuters and malignants; and I have ever observed neuters to turn malignants upon such occasions."

The Second Campaign

In December 1643, in the dead of darkest winter, the Royalists attacked. None were ready for them. Few would have reckoned the chances of an invading army, tramping along the notoriously muddy and water-logged Sussex roads. But the weather was bitterly cold, for days the temperature failed to rise above freezing. In an act that was both bold and daring, General Hopton marched his men over the frozen roads from Petersfield, and across the Downs. At South Harting, the small garrison, after a valiant defence was forced to surrender. Cowdray, Midhurst and Petworth all fell to the Royalist onslaught. On 6 December, forces under the command of Sir Edward Bishop, and the recently knighted Sir Edward Ford, captured Arundel, and laid siege to the castle.

From the point of view of the parliamentarians, the situation was far more grave than it had been a year earlier. Ralph Hopton's army was no militia, but a battle hardened force of Cornishmen and Irishmen, who had decisively beaten William Waller in Devon. At first Parliament could only act with gestures. They appointed John Baker of Mayfield as High Sheriff of Sussex, but his influence in the west of the county was as limited as Sir Edward Ford's was in the east. Once again all hopes lay on Colonel Morley, who decided, following skirmishing on the Downs south of Parham, that the expedient policy was to hold the Adur against a Royalist advance. The town and castle at Bramber were held by a garrison, commanded by twenty-three year old Captain James Temple, who despite overwhelming odds repulsed a Royalist attack on 12 December. The Royalist commanders, perhaps not wishing to sustain unnecessary losses, would have been content to bide their time for the odds were heavily stacked in their favour. Later that same day, reinforcements entered Bramber from Lewes, these included the Puritan preacher Dr. Cheynell, who wrote of his meeting with Captain Temple -

"Upon the 12th of December I visited a brave soldier of my acquaintance, Captain James Temple, who did that day defend the fort of Bramber against a bold and daring enemy to the wonder of all the country; and I did not marvel at it, for he is a man that hath his head full of stratagems, his heart full of piety and valour, and his hand as full of success as it is of dexterity."

Just as at Haywards Heath the year before, the parliamentarians had snatched victory from the jaws of defeat. Now once again the tables were turned. News reached Hopton, that his old friend and adversary William Waller, had attacked the Royalist stronghold of Alton in Hampshire. Hopton was forced to retreat with the bulk of his army back into Hampshire, leaving a garrison of two thousand men at Arundel. The retreat was all in vain, the following day Alton fell to Waller.

On 17 December, the frost still holding, Waller marched out of Farnham, and on the evening of 19 December he was camped within a mile of Arundel. On his way his men captured and ransacked Cowdray, the home of the Catholic Viscount Montagu; he also re-took Harting. From the east came Colonel Morley, with a formidable array of fighting men, some of whom had come from as far away as Rye, and were commanded by no less a person

Arundel Castle & town 1642 (WSCC)

than the mayor himself. By the time the East Sussex contingent reached Arundel they numbered some 4,000 men, added to which were the 6,000 men commanded by Waller. The Royalist garrison was therefore outnumbered by about five to one.

The town fell easily to Waller. But disaster nearly struck as the General entered the town, as a man stepped forward and aimed his musket at Waller from close range. The weapon failed to fire, and the "perfidious rascal" was seized and shortly afterwards, "deservedly hanged." Once against the Almighty had intervened to protect General Waller, and confound his enemies. Not that the Parliamentarians had it all their own way. From the battlements of the castle Royalist snipers inflicted casualties, killing Lieutenant Colonel Ramsey as he rode his horse into the town. Waller then ordered that two 'saker-drake' canon be hoisted into the tower of St. Nicholas's church, from where they were able to fire directly into the castle, killing and wounding several of the enemy.

Writing to Samuel Jeake at Rye, John Coulton described the unfolding drama -

"[we] took Arundel town with 140 prisoners to boot, whereof 60 [now] bear arms for the Parliament, the rest are sent to London. Our Wiston Cavaliers [a reference to Wiston House to the west of Steyning, held by the Royalists] left the house and fled for their lives, and in their march at Findon left 3 carts laden with plunder, the which we with a party of 12 horse fetched home and refreshed our weary soldiers; these things being done by the Lord's hand..."

On a more domestic note, Coulton adds, "Tell widow Dod I eat and drink with both her brothers William and John, they are very well; only my uncle Pye wants his feather bed to sleep on." As the siege continued, so the harsh weather broke, and milder, wetter conditions replaced it. Within the castle, conditions were poor - food was low, and the Parliamentarians had succeeded in poisoning or blocking the supply of water to all but one of the castle's wells. The besieged garrison was not without hope however, Hopton, they believed would come to their rescue. Hopton, at Winchester, was waiting for word from Richard Smith, his spy in Waller's army. Smith had drawn maps to show where the Parliamentarians were camped, and had noted information, including numbers of men, horse and weaponry. Such information would have greatly assisted Hopton in making sound plans for a counter-attack. Smith however was challenged as he tried to leave the confines of the Arundel encampment. He was searched, and a letter actually addressed to General Hopton was found in his jacket. Next morning, on the bridge at Arundel in full view of the castle, he was hanged.

The death of Smith was the least of Hopton's worries, fighting had broken out within the ranks of his own army, between the Cornishmen and the Irishmen. The Cornish contingent were the losers, several of their number being killed or wounded. Dejected, and far away from home, upwards of 1500 of Hopton's Cornishmen deserted his colours, and returned to Cornwall.

Finally, with order restored, on 29 December, Hopton once more marched eastwards. Waller, leaving only 1500 men to continue the siege of Arundel Castle, marched to meet his old adversary. Following skirmishes at South Harting and West Dean, the two armies faced each other on North Marden Down. After a few exchanges of shots, Hopton, seeing the extent to which he was outnumbered, retreated towards Havant. On learning the grim news, the Arundel castle garrison became eager to agree terms of surrender.

At midnight on 5 January 1644, Waller sent an ultimatum to the garrison, stating that Sir Edward Ford and Sir Edward Bishop had to surrender themselves at once if they wished the siege to end without bloodshed. At 2am the two men gave themselves up, and at 9am, the castle was formally occupied by the Parliamentary forces. One thousand prisoners were taken (many had previously deserted the castle, and surrendered), along with 200 horses, 2,000 weapons, 20 barrels of gunpowder, several oxen, and £4,000. The condition of the prisoners was pathetic, one witness to the surrender wrote - "I never saw so many weak and feeble creatures together in my life, for almost all the common soldiers were half starved, and many of them hardly able to set one foot before another." The Royalist cause in Sussex was over.

The extent to which the war in Sussex was seen very much as a county affair, can be judged from the response Waller received from the gentry in the east, as well as the west of Sussex, when he attempted to raise men and money for a continued campaign against the Royalists in Hampshire. With the exception of Colonel Morley, and some of the more zealous sections of the puritan gentry, the response was decidedly lukewarm. Waller was exasperated, and his sense of resentment showed, when he later commented, " I would not have anything to do with the gentlemen of Sussex from whom I have received nothing but constant incivilities." One of Waller's last acts in Sussex was to order the destruction of Bramber Castle, an act that demonstrated his lack of faith in the local gentry.

Remains of Bramber Castle

The Club Men

No town in Sussex suffered during the civil war more than Arundel. Within little over a year it had been plundered, and counter-plundered on two occasions. In 1645, the burgesses grovelled to the parliamentary committee, based at Billingshurst, in a manner which sought to lay all the blame for their reduced circumstances on the Royalists -

"Humblie sheweth: that which your eyes have heretofore seene, and your ears heard, the sad and distressed estate of us, the poore, plundered, robed and spoyled inhabitants of the said burrough, whoe were driven by the kings forces from house and habitation, to secure our lives, and, in our absence, robed and spoyled of all outward comforts to mayntayne a livelihood; some of our houses being burnte, and others made stables of, and some pulled downe, and all our goods imbeasled, and taken away, to our great impoversing."

The committee system replaced the old system of local government based on the Quarter Sessions. The Billingshurst committee was subordinate to the Grand Committee at Lewes, chaired by Sir Thomas Pelham. Eventually some financial re-dress was given to the people of Arundel, but the simmering anger felt in the western rapes continued. Both gentry and peasants wished for a return to the old days, when neither soldiers nor committee men had say over local affairs. Even the Earl of Northumberland,

The ruins of Arundel Castle, prior to restoration (WSCC)

Lord Lieutenant of Sussex, complained that the committee men at Petworth were, "of soe base a condition as renders them unworthy of such trusts." In part this complaint is no more than snobbery, Northumberland was not used to seeing smaller farmers and tradesmen in positions of authority. General Waller had no sympathy for the neutralism still pursued by many of local gentry, "we shall take them," he wrote in April 1644, "for no other than enemies to the State, and men accordingly to be proceeded against."

The plundering of farms and shops by Parliamentary soldiers continued throughout 1645, as did the conscription of local men into the army - both of which were greatly resented. At Nuthurst, villagers killed two soldiers they believed to have been guilty of "rapes and other outrages." A contemporary witness at Horsham wrote that the soldiers were guilty of thieving from the country people, who were then taxed by the "unmerciful" committees -

" When plundering troops killed all the poor countrymen's sheep, these unmerciful people would force excise out of them for those very goods which the others robbed them of; insomuch that the religious soldiers said they would starve before they would be employed in forcing it, or take any of it for their pay."

No name aroused greater hostility amongst the puritans of Sussex than that of 'Lewkenor'. Although belonging to the class of Chichester merchants usually considered stalwarts of the Parliamentary cause, as well as being a member of the Long Parliament, Christopher Lewkenor was a Royalist. When his nephew John was stopped by soldiers and asked his name, he gave an honest reply, upon which the soldiers kicked and beat him, robbed, and stripped him. Such conduct appalled the more genuinely religious Parliamentarians, the committee men expressing their "sorrow", at what they none-the-less insisted on calling an "accident".

It was the persistent attempts to impress local men into the army, which finally led in September 1645, to a great outburst of anger from the poor of western Sussex. The labourers who had been forced to march with Edward Ford in 1642, were now being conscripted into the Parliamentary cause. Armed with wooden bludgeons, from which they gained the name 'club men', the labourers set upon the press gang near Chichester, leaving "sometimes a constable or tithyingman with the blood running around his ears." Of the 67 men due to be imprest in the rape of Chichester, forty were rescued.

On 17 September several hundred club men assembled on Duncton Down. From here they marched on Walberton where an encampment was made. Rumours spread that Clubmen from not just Walberton, but from western Sussex generally, planned to meet at Bury Hill, and then rise up against the occupying forces. At emergency meetings of the Grand Committee at Lewes on the 18 and 19 September, it was reported by William Cawley that 1,000 Clubmen were massing on the Downs outside the city. The Committee ordered Colonel Norton to march into the troubled areas, where he was to be reinforced by the trained bands and the garrison at Arundel Castle. By sheer scale of numbers, and an overwhelming military presence, the club men were overawed; although the men at Walberton remained firm. Still fearing a general rising, Colonel Morley, acting with his younger brother William, then governor of Arundel, launched a dawn raid on the Walberton encampment. Faced with a well armed force, both on foot and horse, the ill-prepared club men could offer little resistance, and were dispersed. For the time being at least order had been restored.

Trouble flared up again in 1648, not in Chichester and Arundel rapes, but in the rape of Bramber, principally around the Horsham area. This time however the protests came not just from the common people, but also from the gentry. Many landed families had been alienated by fines imposed on them for having contributed men to Edward Ford's army in 1642, even though most had supported Ford, oblivious of his true intentions. The continued presence of military garrisons in towns such as Horsham was viewed as both an intrusion and a burden. Even in the east of the county, voices of protest were being raised. Sir John Culpeper of Wakehurst Place at Ardingly became the unofficial spokesman for the dissenting voices, and presented their petition at Westminster. The petitioners asked that -

"No garrisons within the said county be any longer continued and that the ordinance and ammunition taken from the sea townes may be returned for the better defence of them and the whole country from foreign invasion."

Despite the opposition of Herbert Morley and others on the Grand Committee, the demands of the petitioners were conceded, and the military garrisons in the towns of west and central Sussex were removed, allowing Sussex to return to some degree of normality.

The failed Royalist uprising in the west of England in 1651, led to the flight of the twenty-one year old Prince Charles (his father the King had been executed two years earlier), following various adventures and close calls, from Shoreham harbour. The pride in which west Sussex people, and Shoreham people in particular, recalled that dramatic escape found expression on 'Oak Apple Day', 29 May, when right up until the second world war, patriotic people would commemorate Charles's birthday, by wearing oak leaves and oak apples in their lapels.

The long-term repercussions of the civil war in Sussex were considerable. Although the monarchy was restored in 1660, the bitterness of the war years lingered on for several generations. In 1679, the strongly Protestant Duke of Monmouth visited Chichester, and was greeted with bonfires and the ringing of bells by his supporters. Opponents of the Duke, including eighty-three year old Bishop Carelton regarded the visit as tantamount to treason. In the enthusiasm of the visit, a mob attacked the Bishop's Palace, shouting out that the Bishop was an 'old Popish rogue'. The political polarisation of the city into 'Tory' supporters of the King, and 'Whig' supporters of Parliament became very marked at this time. Violent assaults, including murder, resulted from clashes between the two rival factions. Not until the eighteenth century did the wounds slowly begin to heal, as gradually the wealth and standing of the city was restored.

Arundel, the town that suffered most from the fighting, was still in a sorry state of dilapidation fifty years later. Not until the days of the eighth Duke of Norfolk was both town and castle re-built (the present-day castle is very recent indeed, see under 'Arundel' in the gazetteer). This Duke re-imposed the authority of his ancestors, establishing Arundel as a bastion of the Tory cause in Sussex. By the middle years of the eighteenth century, no less than eight local Members of Parliament were in the 'pocket' of the Duke.

Lewes on the other hand remained under the control of the Pelhams. A descendant of Sir Thomas Pelham, also called Thomas, was created Duke of Newcastle in 1715. He became one of the most powerful men in England, even becoming Prime Minister towards the end of George II's reign. His estates were vast, and by his death in 1768 included the whole of Ashdown Forest, which had been 'enclosed' by Act of Parliament. Just like the Duke of Norfolk in the west of the county, Newcastle ensured that the parliamentary representation in his part of the county remained in the Whig interest.

At Rye, the town continued to decline economically, not because of the war, but due to the silting up of its harbour. The puritan fervour of Jeake and Coulton was replaced by the oligarchy of the Lamb family and their associates, who ran the town as a personal fiefdom throughout the eighteenth century.

The political violence of the seventeenth century had therefore been transformed into institutionalised corruption by the eighteenth century, in which the great landed interests re-asserted their control. Gone were the high ideals of Herbert Morley, and gone also was the solidarity of the old Sussex gentry. For the ordinary people of Sussex, the ebb and flow of political fortune counted for little, for them the great changes would come at a later date, when first the turnpike roads, and then the railway, would transform the life of the county.

As a final thought, the author notes that at the 1997 general election, West Sussex remained staunchly Conservative, while East Sussex proved far more rewarding for the opposition. At Chichester, Horsham, and Arundel, the Conservative majorities were some of the largest in the country, while at Lewes, a Liberal Democrat was elected, with Brighton and Hastings returning Labour candidates. So, perhaps the political differences between the east and west of Sussex still lives on, over three hundred and fifty years after the civil war ended?

BRIGHTON & LEWES

For centuries, the small fishing village of Brighthelmstone lived in the shadow of Lewes, the county town of East Sussex. Then in the middle of the eighteenth century the position was reversed, and fashionable Brighton overtook its ancient neighbour. It is ironic that the man who set Brighton on its new course as a seaside resort, was a resident of Lewes, Dr. Russell. Attempts by Lewes to regain its position came to nothing, and by the middle years of the nineteenth century, Lewes had come to accept the dominance, if not the pre-eminence of its seaside rival. Indeed Lewes people began to be proud of their traditions and their history, and the very fact that their town symbolised the heritage of the county, while Brighton, with its 'London-on-Sea' image, represented the new face of Sussex.

Lewes

Augustus Hare found peace and solitude at Lewes, he also found a healthy population, not something that could be said of many Sussex towns at the time - "The quaint, healthy old town has a lower death rate than any other in England except two. 'Proud Lewes and poor Brighthelmstone' is a proverb of the days when letters were addressed, 'Brighthelmstone near Lewes.' The old houses straggle along the terraces and ridge of a hill which is crowned by the castle tower. At the foot of the hill flows the sluggish Ouse ..."

Fifteen years later, in 1909, Arthur Becket was so struck by the slow pace of life in Lewes, that he remarked to an old inhabitant of the place that his town was dead, to which the old man responded that anyone who said such a thing did not know Lewes. By this he meant that Lewes lived on through its history and its traditions, and in particular its unequalled celebrations of Bonfire Night, which at one time amounted to a yearly riot of flame and cudgel. Lewes today has changed little in appearance, but the incessant flow of traffic through its narrow streets (and this despite a by-pass built in the early 1980's), means that any sense of torpor can only be experienced in the back streets, or in the early hours of the morning.

Lewes Castle in the 18th century (WSCC)

With the exception of a small stretch of road leading up to Cliffe Bridge, Lewes, unlike Chichester, has not benefited from pedestrianisation, a painful fact all too apparent to those who visit these two contrasting county towns.

From the time of the Norman Conquest, the de Warrene family ruled this part of Sussex for two hundred and fifty years, until the death of John de Warrene, who died without legitimate heir during the reign of Edward II. Lewes Castle is well preserved, as is its fine barbican gatehouse, which stands just off the High Street. The Castle is owned by the Sussex Archaeological Society, which operates a well-stocked bookshop in Barbican House, which is close at hand. Anyone wishing to be kept up to date with the latest research regarding the history of Sussex should join the Society, membership of which brings with it a free copy of the Sussex Archaeological Collections, a prestigious journal which was first published in 1847.

Pelham House, owned since 1928 by East Sussex County Council, was built around 1579 by the free-spending George Goring, who was also responsible for building the house at Danny (see p70). The Gorings used the property as a town house. From 1620-1628, another George Goring was a Member of Parliament for Lewes. However the Gorings' staunch support for the King during the Civil War did not go down well in Protestant Lewes, and by 1649, the house had come into the possession of the Pelhams, who gave their name to the house. In the next century the Pelhams, as Dukes of Newcastle, were some of the most powerful men in the land, with estates and interests all over the country. During the nineteenth and early twentieth centuries Pelham House, having been in the ownership of only two families, changed hands many times. One of the most memorable occupants being the Brighton brewer, Ebenezer Robins. In 1926 a city stockbroker, William Taylor Banks became the last private owner of Pelham House, and two years later he sold it to the County Council. Until 1973, Pelham House remained the council's administrative centre, but local government reorganisation enhanced its responsibilities, and new offices, wholly out of keeping with Lewes were built in that year. Pelham House is still in use however, with Full Meetings of the council still taking place in the wood-panelled chamber.

Southover Grange was also built in the reign of Queen Elizabeth. The Caen limestone came from the ruins of Lewes Priory, which had been closed a century earlier as part of Henry VIII's less than pious conversion to the Protestant Reformation (see p50). The first occupant of the Grange was William Newton, and the house remained in the ownership of his family until 1860. Southover developed as a suburb of Lewes following the growth of Lewes Priory, dedicated by William de Warrene. Southover had its own form of local government, which by Victorian times had come to be seen as both inefficient and corrupt. Power rested with the 'Bailiff', who was invariably a member of the Newton family, and often called 'William'.

From 1630-1637, John Evelyn, who was related to the Newtons lived at

Southover Grange in 1903 (WSCC)

Southover Grange while attending Lewes Grammar School. He later became famous as a diarist and man of letters. During the late eighteenth century Colonel William Newton was a close friend of the Prince of Wales, later the Prince Regent, later King George IV. It is believed that on some of his visits to the Grange, George was accompanied by his 'wife', the Roman Catholic, Maria Fitzherbert (see p96) The Prince, who believed himself to be a accomplished horseman, and once claimed to have ridden from Brighton to London and back again in ten hours, nearly lost his life on one visit to the Newtons. He was racing his carriage through Lewes High Street, and took the left hand turn down Keere Street, to the Grange. This was and is the steepest street in Lewes, and the Prince was very fortunate not to crash with fatal consequences.

The last Newton at the Grange found himself in bitter dispute with some of his fellow residents, and in particular a local publican, who allowed the effluent from his brewery to flow down hill to the Grange, where it gathered in fuming pools. The days of the Bailiff of Southover and the Newton hegemony were numbered. Before the century was out Lewes was incorporated, and Southover became just one of the wards in the new Borough. In 1871 the new owner of the Grange, William Laird Macgregor substantially rebuilt and altered the house, but on the work being completed Macgregor took a great dislike to it, and sold the house shortly afterwards. Like Pelham House it went through several owners in quick succession until in March 1945 it was purchased appropriately enough by the Borough of Lewes.

Bull House in the High Street is a timber-framed building dating from the fifteenth century, and owned by the Sussex Archaeological Society. It is most famous as having been the home for nearly eight years of Thomas Paine, later famous for his radical writings. Paine, who was born in Thetford in Norfolk came to Lewes to work as an Excise officer, a profession both despised and poorly paid (see p125) Paine also worked for his landlord at Bull House, which in those days was a tobacconist. It was at the Headstrong Club, a debating society at the White Hart, where Paine first made his mark as an able and persuasive advocate. His first pamphlet was an appeal to the government, calling for better pay and conditions for those working for the Excise service. Paine was

*Bull House, former home of
Thomas Paine*

not thanked for his efforts, and marked down as a trouble-maker. Worse still, the tobacconist shop went out of business, and Paine was in danger of losing both his sources of income. Not wishing to remain in England as a pauper, in 1774 he took the bold step of emigrating to the American colonies.

In America Paine quickly took up the cause of the colonists against the British Government, and published the case for American independence in a trenchant little booklet entitled 'Common Sense.' He later went to France, during the Revolution there, and was elected to the National Assembly. His book 'The Rights of Man' became a source of inspiration to radicals throughout Europe and America. During the Terror in France, Paine was arrested and sentenced to death for his opposition to the execution of the King and members of the Royal Family. He was fortunate in escaping with his life, and fled back to England, where he was regarded as a dangerous revolutionary. His last major work, 'The Age of Reason', was denounced as a blasphemous atheistic tract, and made him particularly unpopular. His last days were spent in America, where he died a pauper's death in drunken obscurity. The American leaders Paine had helped bring to power all deserted him. Although there is a commemorative plaque on Bull House to Paine, it is a great pity that Lewes has never seen fit to build a more substantial memorial to one of the western world's most original and enlightened thinkers.

Lewes House, also in the High Street, is a fine Georgian building, that is today owned by Lewes District Council. In the early twentieth century it was the home of the archaeologist, John Marshell, and the American antiquarian, E. P. Warren. The two men, who always referred to each other by the pet-name, 'Puppy', were both members of a small artistic and literary group devoted to 'Hellenic ideals of manhood'. It was Warren who commissioned the famous sculptor, Rodin to make a full-scale version of his statue, 'The Kiss', which showed two naked lovers embracing. Warren was particularly insistent that the man's genitals should be fully shown, and that no concessions should be made to prudery. In 1904 the eight foot high stone statue was delivered to Lewes House, and there it stood in the hallway for ten years.

On the outbreak of the Great War, Warren donated the work to the people of Lewes, and for three years it stood in the foyer of the Town Hall. There were however many who were shocked by the eroticism of the sculpture, and according to Lewes journalist, John May, a local headmistress and spinster by the name of Miss Fowler Tutt led a campaign for its removal. She succeeded, and an embarrassed council, returned the statue to Warren in 1917, feigning that the Town Hall, "did not lend itself to such a noble piece of statuary." After warren's death, 'The Kiss' eventually found its way to the Tate Gallery. To mark the Millennium celebrations, the Tate will be loaning the controversial work back to Lewes for six months, where it will stand once again on public view in the Town Hall - local spinsters permitting!

Also in the High Street is **Shelleys Hotel**, once an Elizabethan inn known as the Vine. During the eighteenth century it was a private home owned by the Shelley family, whose famous son, Percy Bysshe Shelley often visited his aunts there in the early nineteenth century. It became a hotel in 1946, and for many years was run as a family business. There was much excitement at the hotel one afternoon in the 1950's, when Marilyn Monroe, and her then husband, Arthur Miller, popped in for tea and cakes.

Also in the High Street is the **Old Grammar School**, which was founded in 1519 by Thomas Blunt, who endowed the school with an annual legacy of £3. By 1965 numbers attending the school had dwindled to a mere 35, but the increasing attraction of a private education to middle class parents caused numbers to increase to 330 by the late 1970's, and today (1998) stands at about 400. The prefix 'old' was added to distinguish the school from the state-run Grammar School opened in Lewes in the early twentieth century.

The **Anne of Cleves House** in Southover High Street is yet another property owned by the Sussex Archaeological Society, and one of their most frequently visited. Anne of Cleves never actually lived there, and her connection with the house is the same as with the other 'Cleves' house at Ditchling (see p71)

The name of the Snowdrop Inn at Cliffe dates from 1836, and owes its name not to the pretty little flower of the countryside, but to a terrible tragedy. A Lewes newspaper of that year introduced the news item in suitably sombre tones - "Never before has it fallen to our lot, as recorders of public events, to lay before our readers the particulars of an occurrence similar to that which has been the means this week of casting over our town a universal gloom and sorrow."

December 1836 had seen unprecedented falls of snow and freezing conditions. Short journeys took hours to complete, and longer journeys were made quite impossible, with banks of snow several feet deep accumulating in the valleys. On top of the great chalk cliff at Lewes, which gives its name to the town's eastern suburb, a massive wall of snow hung precipitously, jutting out over the cottages below in Boulder Row. The danger of the situation was apparent to many, and the landlord of the Schooner beer-shop tried to persuade the people to leave their homes. Many however, including eighty-year-old William Geer refused. Mother of eleven, Mary Taylor agreed to leave, taking her children with her. She returned however for a shawl to wrap her youngest in - it cost her life, for at that very moment a massive avalanche of snow came crashing down on the cottages, causing them to collapse. Eight people died, including William Geer, and thirty-year-old Susan Haywood who was trying to persuade the old man to leave.

During the rescue operation, disaster nearly struck again, as another avalanche came down on Boulder Row, burying fifteen of the rescuers. Distraught women dug at the snow with their bare hands, and managed to free all the men, none of whom had sustained serious injury. From the wreckage of the cottages themselves were brought out seven survivors, including three children. On the site of the cottages, the Snowdrop Inn was built, as a permanent reminder of England's only known fatal avalanche. The victims were buried at South Malling Church, where a marble tablet on the north wall commemorates the sad events of December 1836.

Harveys Brewery, which stands by the River Ouse is one of only two remaining independent brewers in Sussex (the other being King and Barnes at Horsham). In 1960 the brewery was nearly washed away when the river burst its banks, and the building was flooded with water, four feet deep. Ninety years earlier, Harveys had used river water for making beer when the local well became infected with the typhus virus. The resulting brew was not one easily forgotten, for at the bottom of his glass, each drinker found a thick residue of muddy silt! Harveys beer is certainly mud-free today, and some of its special brews, including one named after Tom Paine, are very popular with real ale connoisseurs.

After Hastings, the most important battle fought in Sussex was the one at Lewes in 1264. On one side stood the forces of Henry III, and on the other rebellious Barons led by Simon de Montfort. The rebels wanted the King to govern with greater respect for their interests, and had summoned a Parliament to legitimise their actions. De Montfort was a determined and charismatic leader, who for a few short months became King in all but name. His greatest triumph was at Lewes, where his army was victorious. Over the years victims of the fighting have been unearthed at Lewes, the most recent being in 1994 following the development of the former primary school in Spital Lane. One body had a hand missing, another had a deep cut to the jaw, and two had deep cuts to the skull. Others had been buried with their hands behind their backs, suggesting they had been executed after the battle.

Historically Lewes has been identified as a strongly Protestant town, ever since Protestant Martyrs were burned at the stake here during the reign of 'Bloody Mary' in the 1550's (see p.52-54) That tradition is still recalled in the annual Fifth of November celebrations still held in the town. Even in the middle years of the nineteenth century, a strong sense of anti-Catholicism was still keenly felt in the town. In 1857, Protestant rioters disrupted the funeral service of a young Anglo-Catholic woman, who had been a member of the Order of St.

Margaret, based at East Grinstead. The founder of the Order, the Rev. John Neale (see p61) was attacked and chased through the streets of the town by a murderous mob. As recently as 1913, 'Bonfire Boys' at Lewes burned an effigy of a priest. Indeed 'the Pope' is still burnt, although the organisers insist this is simply traditional, and does not represent an image of the present pontiff. The same explanation is given for the large 'No Popery' banner hung across Cliffe High Street each year. Sadly, recent interventions by the Police have robbed Lewes of much of its former spontaneity, and the town is now overwhelmed on 'the Fifth' by visitors who know little about and care even less for the origins of this old festival.

Brighton

Brighton, and its neighbour Hove, are apparently no longer part of the county. As you pass the University of Sussex, heading east on the A27, you will notice a sign, informing you that you are entering 'East Sussex'. This must be very confusing for visitors, and perplexing for residents, and is a result of Brighton and Hove becoming a 'unitary authority', that is to say an authority with both the powers of a borough and a county. There is in fact nothing very new about this, Brighton was a 'county borough' for nearly a hundred years up until the local government re-organisation of 1973. During that time no one pretended it had ceased to be part of East Sussex. Whether these new signs are the result of pique on the part of East Sussex, or excessive vanity on the part of Brighton and Hove it's hard to say, but they are clearly a nonsense and a terrible waste of public money.

There are those who would argue that Brighton has never really been part of Sussex, since it first became the playground of wealthy Londoners in the eighteenth century. The town was certainly transformed by the arrival of sea-bathers, coupled with the excesses and extravagances of the Prince of Wales (later Prince Regent, later King George IV) and his 'court' at the **Royal Pavilion**. Prior to 1750, Brighton was a decaying and declining fishing town, with a population of well under a thousand. Mighty storms in 1703 and 1705 had washed much of the town away and caused a great loss of life. Fifty years on, the town had not recovered, and was still in the doldrums. It may have continued to decline, had it not been for the timely intervention of Dr. Richard Russell of Lewes.

Coastal erosion at Brighton C. 1750 (WSCC)

Dr. Russell was a well-established physician when he published his, 'Dissertation on the Use of Sea Water in the Diseases of the Glands.' This work, written in Latin was not meant for a wide readership, and might well have gathered dust on various library shelves in sundry medical colleges, had it not been for the chance of circumstance. The publication coincided with the increasing popularity of 'health spas', and the connecting of London and Brighton by the construction of a 'turnpike' road - the first properly constructed road built in Sussex since Roman times. By the time of his death in 1759, Russell had established a thriving practice at Brighton, offering people the opportunity of benefiting from the 'Sea Cure.' Russell's original premises were on the site of the present-day **Royal Albion Hotel**. On the south side of this building, suitably facing the sea, is a commemorative plaque to Russell, which simply states: 'if you seek his monument, look around', an appropriate tribute to the founder of modern Brighton.

Russell had observed that Brighton's fisherwomen had, "generally white teeth and firm gums", due he believed to their close proximity to the sea. "The omniscient creator of all things," declared Russell, "has designed the sea to be a kind of common defence against the corruption and putrefaction of bodies." The lifestyle and habits of the eighteenth century aristocracy ensured a plentiful supply of patients for Russell and his successors. Many of them may not have been fully prepared for the full rigours of the therapy however, for the treatment entailed drinking sea water as well as bathing in it. Indeed Russell warned that, "Many persons are apt to hurry into a course of bathing before the body is altered and sufficiently prepared by drinking sea-water, or by a previous course of other remedies; which hurry is always detrimental to the patient by protracting his cure."

The produce of the sea was also prescribed by Russell for the elevation of various maladies. Seaweed and other sea plants were recommended for the treatment of skin complaints. Russell had them baked, dried and powdered before they were administered, by applying them to hot coals - the vapours given off being 'funnelled' onto the patient's skin. Special fomentations of sea-water would have been administered prior to the vapours. All Russell's 'medicines' were of course available at no cost to himself, although the cost to his patients, both financially, and, we may think, physically, were considerable. His reputation remained unsullied for many years. In 1818, nearly seventy years after his death, it was said that the leading families of Sussex still kept prescriptions, written by Russell, and regarded them with 'veneration'.

One of Russell's successors equalled and even surpassed his fame and fortune. Sake Dean Mahomed, a Persian sailor, married to an Irish wife, established his 'Vapour and Shampooing Baths' at Brighton in 1786. In those days 'shampooing' did not have its modern meaning, but consisted of a vigorous massage in the atmosphere of a Turkish bath. Amidst the 'creaking of bones', Mahomed established a reputation for being able to cure complaints even the great doctor would have thought beyond his powers. Asthma, contractions, paralysis, rheumatism, sciatica, lumbago, and loss of voice, were amongst the ailments Mahomed claimed to have cured. To the sceptical, he would show his 'museum' of crutches, spine-stretchers, leg-irons, head-strainers, bump-dressers, and club-foot reformers, all discarded over the years, he assured the visitor, by his former patients. Mahomed attended to the rich and famous of his day, including the Prince. He lived to be 101, and his gravestone can still be found in St. Nicholas' Church.

The Prince first came to Brighton when he was 21 in 1784. Some accounts say he came to visit his licentious uncle, the Duke of Cumberland, others that he came to be 'cured' of a stiff neck. Whatever the reason for coming, the Prince was taken with Brighton, and returned the following year. A local news-paper in June 1785 described George's antics in the town -

"His Royal Highness amused himself on the Steyne for some time in attempting to shoot doves with single balls; but with what result we have not heard, though the Prince is esteemed a most excellent shot, and seldom pre-sents his piece without doing some execution. The Prince, in the course of his diversion, either by design or accident, lowered the tops of several of the chim-neys of the Hon. Mr. Windham's house."

A view of Brighton 1785 (looking west) (WSCC)

In 1787 work began on plans for a house for the Prince, to be built on the Steine. This building would eventually become the Royal Pavilion, and cost the Prince, or rather his father, over a million pounds to build. Although regarded as quintessentially Brighton today, it was once held to be a vulgar monstrosity.

Queen Victoria refused to have anything to do with her uncle's creation, and eventually bequeathed it, with Royal good riddance to the people of Brighton. Victoria preferred the sedate isolation of Osborne on the Isle of Wight to the bustle of Brighton. George's brother, William, who succeeded him as King in 1830, did continue to use the Pavilion, and took delight in walking on the Chain Pier, built in 1823 (and lost in a storm seventy years later).

Not far from the Pavilion was **Stein House**, the home of Mrs. Fitzherbert, the Prince's true love, and the woman he secretly married. Maria Fitzherbert was older than the Prince, and a widow twice-over. She was also a Roman Catholic, and therefore disbarred by Act of Parliament from marrying an heir to the throne. The Prince had little regard for such trifles and married her anyway. He was later forced into an official marriage with Princess Caroline of Brunswick. It was a loveless union, in fact the couple detested each other. Caroline became very popular with the common people, and there was widespread mourning when she died suddenly in 1820. Although popular in Brighton, the Prince was not popular in England as a whole. The mob stoned his carriage on the day of his coronation. Through all these traumas, Maria Fitzherbert kept a quiet dignity. She outlived her 'husband' by seven years, and died at her home in Brighton.

Brighton is famous for its two piers. As already stated it once had a third pier, lost in stormy seas just over a hundred years ago. Of the two that remain, the **West Pier**, a grade I listed building became unsafe, and has been closed for many years. In 1997 it was announced that funds from the National Lottery would be made available to restore it to its former splendour. It is due to be open again to the public in time for the Millennium celebrations. The **Palace Pier** was built thirty years after the West Pier, and was designed to cater for the thousands of 'day-trippers' that descended on Brighton following the Bank Holiday Act of 1871. With its amusements and 'saucy' image, the Palace Pier came to represent popular Brighton. Richard Jefferies lived at Hove shortly before the Palace Pier was built, when the West Pier still aimed at a more upper class clientele, not that such aspirations impressed Jefferies -

"Most people who go on the West Pier at Brighton walk at once straight to the farthest part. This is the order and custom of pier promenading; you are to stalk along the deck till you reach the end, and there go round and round the band in a circle like a horse tethered to an iron pin, or else sit down and admire those who do go round and round. No one looks back at the gradually extending beach and the fine curve of the shore. No one lingers where the surf breaks - immediately above it - listening to the remorseful sigh of the dying wave as it sobs back to the shore."

Jefferies had no time for 'polite society', and generally preferred walking on the heights of the Downs rather than through busy streets. Yet he did not dislike Brighton, and even approved of the lack of trees in its streets, which allowed the walker to better appreciate the unique character of the town's buildings.

A humerous & observant sketch of Pier promenaders at Brighton C.1870 (WSCC)

His essay on the Western Road offers a vivid glimpse of life in Brighton in the 1880's. Jefferies complains of the deplorable state of the road, "It is the most extraordinary road in the Kingdom for holes," he says, adding that council workmen, employed to fill in the cavities only make matters worse, "when it does get a trifle smooth, when the traffic has begun to run in a groove, then they carefully break it up with pickaxes till the surface is like that of a shoeing smith's rasp."

Jefferies condemns the local authorities for insisting that all the omnibuses (horse-drawn of course in those days) keep exactly to the timetable. Men with stopwatches would stand in 'sentinel' boxes, checking that every vehicle was keeping exactly to time. The crews of buses that failed to keep to the timetable would be fined. The result of such 'tyranny', Jefferies explains were painful to observe -

"Aged ladies unable to move briskly are scarcely on the step before the rude machine starts and were it not for helping hands stretched from the other passengers would fall and perhaps be seriously injured. They are compelled to scramble in or out and I have frequently seen them on the verge of fainting from the fright. Children have to take their chance. It is downright cruelty to the very young and the old and not without danger to the nimble. This matter is a disgrace. As a result the conductors, bullied and fined and worried, turn on the passengers, and their manners are those of brutes. They speak in tones to ladies that ought to procure them a sound thrashing."

Jefferies goes on to describe the sheer volume of traffic using the Western Road, and of how a suggestion of a tramway to alleviate the congestion met with stern disapproval from the residents of Hove -

"This wonderful road has another feature, it is moderately wide at the Hove end where the population is less dense and as it approaches Brighton it gradually narrows like the neck of a hock bottle and the traffic is slowly squeezed up tighter and tighter till on busy days the whole is jammed in the vice. All Brighton, at least all Business Brighton squeezes through this narrow neck once a day; all cabs and flies hurrying to the station follow it, hundreds of private carriages joggle along it. It is the road to everywhere in Brighton. Such is the affection of the place for its dear Western Road that nothing would induce the people to part with it. Some one proposed a tramway imagining it would be welcomed as a convenience, which was to run parallel to the Western Road but in another street. The tramway to go right up to the railway station - a remarkable innovation, for it is one of the peculiarities of Brighton that no line of buses is permitted to come to the station. You must take a fly or walk, there are no public conveyances - the nearest is half a mile distant. London stations proffer a choice of omnibus routes: Brighton station has no bus, and poor people must trudge through rain and storm. The tramway was to go up to the station and looked a very convenient arrangement but the Hove people who were chiefly interested would have nothing to do with it. They howled it down, they organised bands of work people to shout it off the platform, and stirred themselves into bubbling indignation. A tramway in sacred Hove - trams in the Holy land of Hove!"

Richard Jefferies

Jefferies despised the prim and proper councillors of Hove, and denounced the new Town Hall, which had cost £40,000 to build - "wrung in part from the poorest population in the world." In his notebook, he jotted down the peculiarities of Brighton and Hove as they occurred to him -

" There are men who obtain a distinction by always doing the same thing - some for example with an arm crossed on their breast as they walk - there is a social distinction in regularity. The ducal descendant who plays the concertina and the beggar who continually moves one foot. The old lady who is muffled up and is always covered with an umbrella. The old gentleman in a bathchair drawn by an ancient, who I am told, has been crippled for thirty years. The old streets on sunny days are picturesque, red tiles, red chimneys, green jalousies, blue sky beyond, shadowy corners and archways. Brick-pavements are very good until worn into holes. The pitchblack houses are disappearing gradually. I dislike the useless old tamarisks scattered about. There is a favourite spot loved by the crowd on the beach just on the west side of the pier. People are many deep here, sitting and reclining."

Richard Jefferies is rightly remembered as a writer of the countryside, yet his commentary on Brighton is of great interest to the social historian. Jefferies left Lorna Road in Hove in 1886, and moved to the then rural quiet of Goring. At only thirty seven his life was ebbing away, and within a year he would be dead.

The first commercially run electric railway in the world was opened on Brighton seafront in 1883. It was the brainchild of local inventor, Magnus Volk, and still runs from just to the east of the Palace Pier, to the Marina, although it once extended all the way to Rottingdean and was conveyed through the waves at high tide on stilts.

In Middle Street is a plaque to William Friese-Greene, who pioneered the world of moving pictures. His popular silent films were shown all over the world in the 1890's and early 1900's, but he was unable to compete with Hollywood, and by the First World War he had been forced out of business. At the height of his success he was famed for his generosity, and was supposed to have regularly given handfuls of bank notes to children begging on the streets. He died in 1921, leaving one shilling and ten pence.

On the periphery of Brighton are found a number of former country houses, now owned by Brighton and Hove Council. **Preston Manor** and Preston Park were left to the then Brighton Corporation by Sir Charles Thomas-Stanford, who was Mayor of Brighton from 1910-1913, and represented the town in Parliament from 1914-1922. In the nave of Preston Church is the grave of Thomas Cheynell, a puritan preacher, prominent during the Civil War (see p80). He lived to see the Restoration, at which time he was barred from preaching. In old age he complained that in Sussex religion was no longer practised nor preached. His old adversaries were somewhat more magnanimous, Bishop Hoadly declaring that Cheynell had been, "as pious, honest and charitable as his bigotry would permit."

On the very northern border of Brighton is **Patcham**, an old-world village lost amidst the sprawl of 1930's suburbia. To the north thunders the recently completed A27 trunk road, and the fairly recently dualled A23. Patcham Place, with its distinctive black-glazed tiles once stood in glorious isolation, looking towards the Downs. Its outlook has certainly changed since it first became a Youth Hostel in 1938. To the north of Brighton, on the route of the South Downs Way is the village of **Pyecombe** - surely the most ruined village in Sussex. High-speed traffic roars by, to both the east and the west. It is hard to believe that this village was once famous for the shepherds' crooks made by the local blacksmith! **Rottingdean**, to the east of Brighton retains some old streets and a village pond, and was once home to Rudyard Kipling. Traditional singer and countryside writer, Bob Copper was born here, as were generations of his family. The Copper family still sing traditional Sussex songs, handed down through generations of their family. Every Christmas the family and their friends perform the traditional 'mummers play' at the pubs in the village.

THE EASTERN DOWNS & PEVENSEY LEVELS
Newhaven and Seaford

Seaford was once an important port and harbour of some antiquity. The church at nearby Southease is one of the oldest in the county, and has a round, Saxon tower. The French made raids on the town during the late medieval period, and were resisted by the townspeople. The town was proud of its status as a Cinque Port. All this came to an end with a series of sixteenth century storms, which resulted in the harbour silting up, and the course of the river being diverted to the village of Meeching, to the west of Seaford. At Meeching a new port or 'New Haven' grew up, and gradually Seaford was superseded.

Seaford Head in 1850: waiting for the detonation (WSCC)

Seaford Head, the high chalk cliffs to the east of the town, has attracted the attention of archaeologists in recent years, who have discovered several remains from the Roman period. In 1850, excavations of a less refined nature took place when the Army detonated high explosives here, demolishing a great section of the cliff. There is a popular walk from Seaford, over the Head, to the Seven Sisters Country Park at Exceat.

The town of Seaford still retains some old streets and buildings, some of which have only altered from their original use in recent years. The town's oldest licensed premises, the Buckle Inn previously the town's oldest licensed premises has now closed and is now a private residence.. About thirty years there was uproar in Seaford when the brewery which owned the Buckle decided to give it a new name. Today such name changes are all too common, and in some places all the old pub names have gone, to be replaced by ridiculous new ones which have no bearing on the locality, either past or present. It is just another example of how our sense of community has been eroded by commercial interests. Back in the 60's and 70's there was still enough sense of local pride in Seaford to ensure that the name of the Buckle was preserved, for it was a name of great historical significance. At the Battle of Poiters in 1356, the local landowner, John de Pelham, captured the King of France, and took the buckle of his belt as a trophy. The King was later released, but the royal buckle remained at Seaford, and became a Pelham family emblem. Although the old inn has now closed, the building is known as 'Buckle House', so at least the historic name survives.

On the subject of inns, there was once a famous beer brewed at Newhaven known as 'Tipper', in memory of its originator, Thomas Tipper, who died, and was buried at Newhaven in 1785. Tipper was a great friend of Thomas Turner (see p117), the Sussex diarist. Turner often visited Newhaven to dine with "my friend Tipper." The inscription on his grave was written by Thomas 'Clio' Rickman of Lewes, a friend of Thomas Paine, who styled himself as a 'Citizen of the World'. One couplet of Rickman's verse declares - "Honest he was, ingenious, blunt and kind; And dared do, what few dare do, Speak his mind." By 1909, when Arthur Beckett was visiting Newhaven, Tipper's life and works may have been forgotten, but his brew had not. At a local pub, Beckett called for a pint of the famous ale, and inquired of its strength and properties -

"...he barman told me that to be perfect, Tipper beer must be kept for seven years. But some time ago one of the great vats at the brewery, in which the beer was kept to mature, burst; and hence most of the 'Tipper' ale drunk nowadays is only about two years old. I found it good at that, the flavour full and pleasant and slightly brackish, though the barman had told me that his customers generally drank it mixed with a milder ale, for 'Tipper' has virtues that are different from those of beers of more modern repute. The said virtues of 'Tipper' are these: a man may drink a glass and be merry, he may drink two glasses and be mighty; but if the little goddess that lurketh in the glass tempteth him to drink a third, and he drink again, then let him go out on to the Downs, and may the Powers that are above, preserve him."

The Newhaven Brewery is no more, and seven-year-old Tipper is but a legend to tease the imagination of Sussex drinkers. Gone also is the Jolly Sailor in Chapel Street, the county's last Beer House (a premises licensed to sell beer and cider only), which closed in 1977. Also lost in that year was the town's old

A Newhaven fisherman with boys 1845

lighthouse, which was demolished. The old Fort, built during the Napoleonic Wars still survives, and has been converted into a leisure centre.

William Coombs, a miller of Newhaven must rank as one of the county's most eccentric personalities. For years he never actually went inside his own mill, but directed operations from the mill's steps. This was all a result of a wager , in which Coombs announced that if he was mistaken in his point of view, he would never enter his own mill again. It was subsequently proved that his opinion was incorrect, and true to his word he never stepped inside his mill again. Coombs' eccentricities were legion for instance he took to colouring his horse, to the incredulity of his neighbours. His wife, Mary, was intolerant of his strange behaviour, and the two led a 'cat and dog' life. Coombs often used to say that a 'voice from heaven' had called down to him on his wedding day, warning him that he would be a miserable man if he married. He would always conclude this anecdote by adding, "And I be a miserable man."

Alfriston

Alfriston is one of those places that tourism chiefs dream of: old, timber-framed buildings line a narrow street, leading to a magnificent parish church, while all around the Downs rise up, to both the east and the west. To complete the picture, the little Cuckmere river meanders unhurriedly through on its way to the sea. Affluence is the other characteristic which pervades today, as it does in all the villages of the South Downs. You would be hard pressed to find any dwelling, however humble, for less than £100,000 (1998 prices), and the old spit and sawdust inn, the Star, is now a very up-market and pricy hotel. It is easy to imagine that things have always been like this at Alfriston, yet less than a hundred years ago, Arthur Beckett remarked that, "Some of the villagers live like poor Irish peasants among their animals." Before the First World War, Downland villages were far from affluent, as families tried to survive on the pitiful wages paid to rural workers in those days. So when Beckett declared, "For me no village of Sussex has greater old-world charms than Alfriston", he was thinking as much of the traditions and customs of the villagers, as he was of the history of its buildings.

Arthur Beckett

Beckett was enthralled by the tales and stories of the poor folk of Alfriston, some of which he retold at length in his book, 'The Spirit of the Downs'. There is the gruesome account of the murder of a young man named Chowne, and his dog, by thieves. The deed took place on the 'White Way', which leads out from the village, and up on to the Downs. Every seven years, on the anniversary of the murder, the ghost of the white terrier dog would appear on the White Way, before vanishing into the earth bank by the side of the road. Anyone seeing the creature would befall a calamity, even death. The haunting only ceased when council workmen, widening the track many years later, discovered the skeleton of Chowne buried in the earth bank. The remains were then reburied in consecrated ground in the churchyard, after which the haunting ceased. During the summer of 1998, this author was recounting this story to a group of walkers on the White Way, when looking up, one of the party noticed a small white dog rummaging in the bank at the side of the track. There was a general sense of relief when its owner appeared over the brow of the hill!

Beckett also relates the legend (for facts are few and far between) of the local smuggler, Stanton Collins, who was active in these parts in the years following Waterloo. Smuggling was very widespread in Sussex during the eighteenth century, and the first forty years of the nineteenth (see pp118-125), and smugglers such as Collins became heroic figures in the eyes of the common people, just as they were demonised by the authorities. Beckett tells of how the Preventive Men would patrol along the cliffs, south of Alfriston, looking out for the illegal landing of contraband. At night they followed a line of chalk rocks, to ensure they did not stray close to the cliff's edge. The smugglers are supposed to have moved the stones, thereby sending at least one officer crashing to his death on the rocks below.

Collins, according to Beckett even involved himself in a local religious dispute. Many of the villagers were non-conformists, and attended the chapel dedicated to the Countess of Huntingdon's Connexion (A denomination that still survives at East Grinstead, see p62). A bitter dispute arose between the minister, the Rev. George Betts and one of his deacons. Among other things, Betts opposed the deacon's wish to marry his deceased wife's sister. Eventually the deacon's supporters seized the chapel, and appointed a new minister. Bett's supporters vowed to fight on, and one Sunday literally forced their way into the chapel -

"Into the galleries and pews they rushed, and only stopped before the pulpit. The stranger parson stood there, pale and trembling, with men on either side of him. There was a row of deacon's supporters in front, and a guard round the communion table. Only a moment the attackers paused to survey the scene, then forward they rushed again. Men were tipped up and trodden upon, women screamed and swooned, and children clung to their mothers' skirts. The pulpit rails were broken up and used as weapons, clothes were torn and blood flowed freely. And old George Betts stood aloof beneath the gallery, pale and powerless, tears of sorrow running down his cheeks."

"The struggle continued, and it seemed as if, after all, the minister's adherents would have to retreat, when, just at this critical juncture, a dozen rough-looking men burst into the chapel. They were smugglers, with Stanton Collins at their head. With a roar they broke through the combatants, pulled down the deacon and preacher from the pulpit, and dispersed the bodyguard. The battle was won."

According to Beckett, "for the rest of the service the smugglers occupied the front row of pews to guard the pulpit against surprise." Collins' intervention made him many enemies in the village, and evidence was provided to the authorities concerning his criminal activities. He was subsequently arrested, tried, and sentenced to be transported to Australia. The supporters of the deacon then took their case to the High Court where they were granted possession of the chapel. Such was the course of brotherly love some one hundred and seventy years ago.

Alfriston's inns are very fine, and the description that Beckett gives of them differs little today, excepting his descriptions of the clientele which has changed absolutely. The pub today called the 'Smugglers' was not so named in Beckett's time and is reputed to have been the home of Stanton Collins. The George and Dragon is probably the old-

Alfriston Church

est of the village's inns, and is known to have existed in the fourteenth century. Not long after, the Star came into being. It is a wonderful building, not least for its strange, intricate and very old carvings, depicting variously, a stag, serpents, a Bishop, probably St. Richard, and St. George. Most striking of all is the large red 'lion', which stands in an alcove at the corner, and is believed originally to have been the figurehead of a Dutch vessel, wrecked off Cuckmere Haven.

Today at the Star you will find guests from all over England, and from many countries overseas, Germans, Americans and Japanese. In fact just about the only accent you will not hear is a South Country one. The dialects and accents of Sussex have just about died out. They were declining even in Beckett's time, but the process was really accelerated after the First World War by the influx of

Londoners into the county, and by the combined effect of the 'wireless' and cinema as well as the influence of compulsory schooling. Stand in the bar of the Star today, or indeed any other similar establishment in Sussex and you will hear little of Sussex or even of farming. How different it was ninety years ago, when Beckett lunched at his "favourite inn" -

"Enter the common room and order a tankard of ale, and make up your mind to be sociable. What is the company? On one of the forms near the long deal table sits a burly farmer, with his coat off and his shirt sleeves rolled up to the elbow, exposing his hairy forearms. Strong and hale and hearty he is. His conversation is of the crops…"

"That old man with the red and wrinkled face, sitting by the window, is a South Down shepherd. He wears the time-honoured smock, reaching to the knees. His half-bred sheep-dog is under the master's bench, as obedient now as when doing his duty on the Downs. The shepherd is a quiet man. His occupation makes silence a habit…"

"The other occupants of the bar," Beckett tells us, "are the blacksmith, one or two tradesmen and a few labourers." And not a visitor, English or foreign to be seen.

As well as the church, often referred to as the 'Cathedral of the Downs', and the old inns, modern visitors to Alfriston should visit the Clergy House, which stands close to the church. It was the first property to be purchased and restored by the National Trust, back in 1896.

Just to the west of Alfriston is **Alciston**. This village was decimated by the Black Death of 1348. Although small today, in pre-plague times it was an important centre of monastic power, being the western outpost of the Battle Abbey estate. The old tithe barn, one of the largest in the country, still survives, as does a medieval dovecote. Easter was once marked in Sussex by communal skipping. This ancient custom was still being observed at Brighton in the

1930's, but did not survive the Second World War. Increasing road-traffic and the lure of modern amusements, gradually eroded this, and many other traditional street festivities. Just before the First World War, 'Long Rope Day' at Newhaven was transferred to Alciston, as the Evening Argus for April 1960 reported -

The Clergy House

"Sleepy Alciston, nestling in the shadow of the Downs, sprang to life yesterday as a 50-year old tradition was observed. The normally quiet street outside the village inn became a seething mass of people waiting to see the traditional skipping ceremony started 50 years ago by a Newhaven family. Most of the watchers had taken the easy way to get to the village - by car, but an enthusiastic band of about 100 had followed the normal practice and walked straight over the Downs from Newhaven, taking nearly three hours. After a break for refreshment, the traditional skipping ceremony with the 20-yard long skipping rope took place with both children and adults joining in while television cameras recorded the ceremony."

Eastbourne

Eastbourne, as a seaside resort was the creation of one man, the seventh Duke of Devonshire, who owned all the land in this part of Sussex. He had inherited the title in 1858, a time when the railway was expanding all across the county. The Duke could see the attractions of Eastbourne as a potential resort, especially with the magnificent promontory of Beachy Head so close at hand. The little village of Eastbourne, which was about a mile inland, nestling in the Downs, sheltering from the sou'westerly winds and the sea spray was not part of the Duke's plans. His new town would be built right by the sea, and so it was, in little more than a decade. Fine terraces and hotels offered a holiday of exclusive refinement to the discerning visitor. By 1871 the 'old town' and its population of no more than a few hundred had been swamped by the 10,000 residents of the 'new town'. In 1883 Eastbourne was granted borough status, by which time its population had risen to 30,000. In 1911 it became a county borough, with a population of over 50,000. No other town in Sussex experienced such rapid growth in the late nineteenth century. After his death in 1891, a great bronze statue of the seventh Duke was erected on Grand Parade - the great benefactor depicted, sitting, craggy faced, contemplating the sea.

The emergence of the Victorian seaside resort did more than anything else to change the way of life in Sussex, and in many other parts of coastal England as well, a theme taken up by The Times in 1860 -

"Our seaport towns have been turned inside out. So infallible and unchanging are the attractions of the

Eastbourne Old Town 1891 (WSCC)

Eastbourne fisherman & women in the 1880's (WSCC)

ocean that it is enough for any place to stand on the shore. That one recommendation is sufficient. Down comes the Excursion Train with its thousands - some with a month's range, others tethered to a six hour limit, but all rushing with one impulse to the water's edge. Where are they to lodge? The old 'town' is perhaps half a mile inland, and turned as far away from the sea as possible, for the fishermen who built it were by no means desirous of always looking at the sea or having the salt spray blowing in at their windows. They got as far back as they could, and nestled in the cliffs or behind the hill for the sake of shelter and repose. But this does not suit visitors whose eyes are always on the waves and so a new town arises on the beach. Marine Terraces, Sea Villas, 'Prospect Lodges', 'Bellevues', hotels, baths, and libraries and churches soon accumulate, till at length the old borough is completely hidden and perhaps only to be reached by an omnibus."

Old Sussex did not always embrace the incomers. Riots and disturbances on Bonfire Night often took on an anti-Londoner flavour, and in the 1880's, there were protests and riots against the arrival of the 'London' Salvation Army in Sussex. The Salvationists, with their evangelical fervour, and the equality they espoused between the sexes, shocked respectable opinion. Many persons in positions of influence and responsibility actively encouraged the 'Skeleton Army' gangs, which broke up Salvation Army prayer meetings, and attacked their street parades. At Eastbourne in 1891, the mayor himself was accused of inciting the mob. Following the example of Worthing in 1884, the disturbances turned to rioting, in which the Police became involved. Unlike Worthing however it did not prove necessary to bring the army onto the streets to impose order.

Southease Church with early twelfth-century round tower

Beachy Head

Beachy Head is the point where the South Downs meet the sea. The chalk cliffs stand 575 ft high, and offer unrivalled glimpses across the sea. This whole magnificent area of downland is owned by Eastbourne Borough Council, which had the foresight back in the 1920's to purchase the land here, and thus protect it from the developers. Unimproved chalk grassland, or 'downland turf' as it is more commonly known, abounds between Eastbourne and Seaford, and is still sustained by flocks of sheep - an increasingly rare sight on the Downs these days. Plans to build a huge hotel, visitors' centre, and other facilities, put forwarded by some misguided individuals in the early 90's, were thankfully

Beachy Head & lighthouse

dropped. The present pub and visitors' centre provided the necessary facilities without damaging the unique setting of Beachy Head.

Richard Jefferies believed he could step back in time on Beachy Head, where, looking out to sea, he could easily imagine a Roman vessel sailing past, so unchanging and timeless was the view. It was the air, at this height, coming as it did from the sea, which most impressed him, and lifted his spirits -

"But the glory of these glorious Downs is the breeze. The air in the valleys immediately beneath them is pure and pleasant; but the least climb, even a hundred feet, puts you on a plane with the atmosphere itself; uninterrupted by so much as the tree tops. It is air without admixture. If it comes from the south, the waves refine it; if inland, the wheat and flowers and grass distil it. The great headland and the whole rib of the promontory is windswept and washed with air; the billows of the atmosphere roll over it."

Two of our Victorian guides had a rather stark disagreement concerning the bird life at Beachy Head. Augustus Hare wrote that, "The chalk cliffs are the refuge of thousands of puffins, guillemots, choughs, razorbills, and other seabirds. Peregrine falcons are seen, and the rare rock-dove - columbia livia - has been found here."

Writing a few years later, W H Hudson was not impressed by Hare's commentary

"Augustus Hare, in his lately-published work, Sussex, speaks of Beachy Head as a haunt of thousands of sea-fowl - puffins. sea-gulls. choughs, etc. Bless the man! He is many years behind the times. On all the fifteen miles of precipitous chalk cliffs extending from Beachy Head to Brighton the only birds to be seen now are those commonest universal cliff-breeders, the herring-gull and jackdaw, and a few kestrels. The one surviving pair of peregrine falcons that haunt this coast have in recent years been annually robbed of their eggs or young."

Hudson goes on to explain the demise of the other varieties of birds once found at Beachy Head -

"It is not possible, said to me a gentleman residing on this south coast a year or two ago, for any man to see a large rare bird and not 'go for it.' The pleasure of shooting it is too great to be resisted, however sorry he may be that all these fine birds are being exterminated throughout the country. If he is not himself a collector he will be sure to have a friend or neighbour who is, and who will be delighted to have a Sussex-killed raven, spoonbill, honey buzzard, or stone curlew sent to him as a present."

Such was the attitude to wild birds in 1899, in the 'good old days', an attitude which persisted until fairly recent times (see Pagham Harbour, p10). The Victorians and Edwardians were renowned for their foolhardy eccentricity, of which this wholesale slaughter appears to have formed a part. Other manifestations of the reckless Englishman at Beachy Head are documented by Arthur Beckett, who mentions men who scaled, or attempted to scale the cliffs at Beachy Head, dressed in their every day clothes, with neither ropes nor picks to help them. One man in 1898, according to Beckett, attempted the ascent with a bicycle on his back!

Just as people have risked their lives in attempting to climb up Beachy Head, so others have been all too willing to end their lives by throwing themselves down the cliffs. Beachy Head has the dubious distinction of being one of the world's suicide blackspots. A local coastguard, talking back in 1978, tried to rationalise the grim work of retrieving the dead. "It is depressing to know you will probably be bringing up a body rather than rescuing someone," he said, adding, "I know many of the bodies are at the bottom of the cliff through choice and in a way that helps."

At the time of writing (July 1998) the future of the Belle Toute lighthouse hangs in the balance. Built in 1831, it stands at the cliff edge, and is in imminent danger of crashing down onto the beach below, as the cliffs here are subject to continual erosion. There is a proposal to dismantle the lighthouse and re-build it elsewhere, but it remains to be seen if the funding will be forthcoming to make such plans a reality. The Belle Toute was replaced in 1903 by the current lighthouse, which stands at the bottom of the cliffs. The new location

An ox-team ploughing the Downs near Beachy Head in 1866 (WSCC)

was chosen because the Belle Toute was often hidden from vessels owing to thick mists and fogs which frequently settled on the cliff tops. The unofficial patron saint of mariners rounding Beachy Heady was the Rev. Jonathan Darby, vicar of East Dean in the early eighteenth century. It was he who created the cave in the cliffs into which shipwrecked seafarers could escape. Once in the cave they could follow steps, hewn into the chalk, which took them to the surface. Nothing of 'Parson's Darby's Hole' now exists, although Beckett says fragments could still be seen in 1909.

Pevensey

Pevensey's castle dominates this little town (or should we say village?). First built by the Romans to protect the coast against pirate raids, it was allowed to fall into dilapidation during Saxon times. The Normans refortified it, and gave the name 'Pevensey' to the administrative division or 'rape' that was created in this part of the county. When Robert de Mortain rebelled against King William II ('William Rufus') in 1088, the loyal William de Warrene of Lewes besieged him. The rebellion was broken, and Mortain fled to Normandy. For a time Pevensey rape was held by the de Warrenes. In 1144, during the wars of 'Stephen and Matilda' the castle was besieged for a second time, and then for a third time during Simon de Montfort's rebellion of 1265 (see p72). The castle was besieged for the last time in 1399, when it was held by the Pelham family, who supported the claims of Henry of Lancaster against those of King Richard II. In her husband's absence, the castle was held by Lady Joan Pelham, whose letter, smuggled out to her husband, is believed to be the oldest surviving correspondence written in English (as opposed to Norman French or Latin). In it she avails her husband of her desperate situation -

"... And my dear Lord, if it like you to know my fare, I am here laid by in manner of a siege with the county of Sussex, Surrey, and a great parcel of Kent, so that I may not [go] out not no victuals get me, but with much hard[ship]. Wherefore, my dear, if it like you by the advice of your wise counsel for set to remedy of the salvation of your Castle and withstand the malice of the shires which have so despitefully wrought to you, and to your Castle, to your men and to your tenants; for this country they have wasted for a great while. 'Farewell, my dear Lord! the Holy Trinity keep you from your enemies, and soon send me good tidings of you."

Lady Joan's prayers were not in vain, and the siege was lifted. More importantly Henry of Lancaster triumphed and became King Henry IV. So was set in train the rise of the Pelham family, a family which was to take control of Sussex during the Civil War (see pp 74-82), and then became one of the most powerful families in England during the following century (see p86)

During the French invasion threat of the early 1800's, 'martello' towers were built along the coast, south of Pevensey, but the castle itself was not refortified. During the Second World War, reinforced concrete 'pill-boxes' were built into the ruined walls, but cleverly disguised with flint and mortar to make them appear part of the original structure. Apart from the castle, Pevensey has two other old buildings of note. The Mint House was once indeed a mint, and claims to be one of the most haunted houses in Sussex. The Court House was once the 'town hall' of the ancient borough of Pevensey, which was abolished by the Great Reform Act of 1832.

Hurstmonceax Castle (FG)

Three miles to the north of Pevensey, across the marshes and water meadows known as the Pevensey Levels is the village of Herstmonceux (sometimes spelt 'Hurstmonceaux'). The name is derived from the de Monceux's, who were granted the lands here during Norman times. A later member of the family fought on Simon de Montfort's side at the Battle of Lewes in 1264 (see p72) The estate later passed, through marriage to the de Fienes family. It was Sir Roger Fienes, who in 1440 began work on the construction of **Herstmonceux** Castle. The innovation employed in the construction of the castle was that it was built of brick rather than stone, and it is generally believed to be the oldest brick building of its size anywhere in the country. Sir Roger's son, Richard, became chamberlain to Elizabeth Woodville, who later married Edward IV. Richard married the only daughter and only surviving child of Lord Dacre. Thus Richard's eldest son inherited the title, Lord Dacre.

The Dacre's neighbours were the ambitious Pelhams. Thomas, Lord Dacre was only twenty-three when he was granted the honour of welcoming Henry VIII's fourth bride, Anne of Cleves to England in 1540. However the marriage was doomed (see p71), and those associated with it were tarnished in the King's eyes. Sir Nicholas Pelham had a large deer park at Hellingly, not far from Herstmonceux. One night in 1541, following a drunken evening with friends, the young Lord Dacre decided to make a raid on his neighbour's deer. However the drunken bawling of Dacre and his companions roused Pelham's keepers, who challenged the aristocratic poachers. A fight took place, after which Dacre and his companions fled, leaving one of Pelham's keepers fatally wounded. Revenge was swift and merciless, Dacre and three of his friends were hanged at Tyburn for murder. Writing over fifty years later, the historian Camden was of the opinion that the prospect of getting hold of the Dacre estates motivated many of those who called for revenge to be exacted. The position of Sir Nicholas Pelham was certainly enhanced by his rival's demise.

In 1708 the castle and estates passed to George Naylor, who was married to the sister of Thomas Pelham, Duke of Newcastle. Their daughter, Grace, is said to have starved herself to death before she reached twenty-one. The estate then passed to her cousin, Francis Naylor, who in turn left the estate to his half-brother, Robert Hare, a Canon of Chichester.

Robert's second wife, Henrietta Henckel, persuaded her husband to demolish the interior of the castle, and use the bricks to build a 'modern' house elsewhere on the estate. From this time on the castle was uninhabited.

Francis Hare inherited the estate from his father. His wife, the beautiful though somewhat eccentric Georgiana, gave birth to four sons, Francis, Augustus, Julius and Marcus, who all made their mark as literary and artistic figures. Augustus Hare, in his own book on Sussex, described the characteristics of Georgiana, and the reason for the Hares departure from Herstmonceux -

Augustus Hare

"Mrs. Hare Naylor, who was famous as a linguist, and insisted on her children conversing in Greek at the family repasts, was as peculiar as she was beautiful. Daily, dressed in white, she rode on a white ass to drink at a mineral spring in the park: a tame white doe ran by her side. One day, at the gate of the park near the church, the white doe was killed by dogs. Then Mrs. Hare Naylor left Hurstmonceaux at once, and never could be persuaded to return there. Thus, in 1807, Francis Hare Naylor sold the estate, and it has since passed through several hands. The living of Hurstmonceaux remained in the Hare family till 1855."

Not surprisingly, given so many traumas, the castle and its grounds are said to be haunted. There is Thomas, Lord Dacre, who rides his horse into the moat, the skeletal apparition of Grace Naylor, and the distraught figure of Georgiana Hare. To these must be added the 'Drummer of Herstmonceux', who is nine foot high, and stands on the castle battlements, beating on his drums, with sparks flying from his drumsticks. Many of these tales are believed to originate with smugglers, who are supposed to have used the abandoned castle as a warehouse for contraband, and therefore wished to scare away the curious.

East of Herstmonceux is **Hailsham**, once known as the 'String Town' due to the rope-making industry based in the town. String was actually known as 'twine' locally. Upper Dicker was home, in the early years of the twentieth century to Horatio Bottomley, financier, publisher, Member of Parliament, and arch rogue and crook, who was gaoled for fraud. The villagers of Upper Dicker never deserted him, and celebrated his release from prison in 1927 with great festivities.

Hailsham Cattle Market C.1870

CRIME & PUNISHMENT

Sussex in 1750 was not, by our standards, a very different place from the one ruled over by Norman lords seven hundred years earlier. It was still over-whelmingly rural, and sparsely populated. Aristocratic landowners dominated everyday life, while the great mass of the population remained poor, and for the most part submissive. The wealden areas alone had a greater tradition of protest, and by the eighteenth century there was plenty to be disgruntled about: old industries were declining, while large areas of common land were being enclosed. The result was a criminal epidemic, made notorious by the activities of smugglers and highwaymen.

It was the arrival of the turnpike roads in the mid to late eighteenth century, followed by the railways in the 1840's and 50's which were to transform Sussex. No longer inaccessible, Sussex attracted the wealthier classes from London to visit its bur-geoning seaside resorts. The railway brought with it London's middle class, and by the 1870's, the working class as well. The process began as a trickle, but developed into a tor-rent, which continued to grow. By the early years of the present century the incomers outnumbered

Smuggler's murder an informer (WSCC)

the indigenous people. The growth of motor traffic from the 1920's onwards turned the torrent into a flood, sweeping away the old Sussex forever. This cultural disaster was also an economic miracle, for it created great affluence in Sussex, and allowed people to live in a manner that their ancestors could not even have imagined.

The eighteenth century saw a rising tide of crime in Sussex, much of it violent. The response to the worsening situation was itself violent, with large numbers of public executions taking place in the county. The years following the end of the Napoleonic Wars in 1815 were some of the worst of all, during which the county seemed in very real danger of degenerating into class war. The great wave of machine breaking and arson which accompanied the Swing riots of 1830, marked the low point. However similar outbreaks, albeit on a smaller scale continued for another generation. In some parts of Sussex, rural terror-ism lingered on until the 1880's. The gradual decline and containment of crime can be explained by the rise of professional law enforcement agencies, such as the Police and the Coastguard, on one hand, and the emergence of the urban economy on the other, which offered new, and for the most part, better paid sources of employment.

The differences between the different geographical areas of Sussex, as far as economic decline and crime area are concerned, were very marked indeed. For most of the period it was the villages of the High Weald that suffered the most, although the great depression of the 1820's and 30's affected the whole county. Even then, there were surprising differences from one parish to another. At Rottingdean in 1830, for instance, there were no riots, no outbreaks of arson, and no machine breaking. The reason, appears to lie with the local landowning family, who went to considerable lengths to ensure that the labourers on their estate were properly provided for, and that wages were not cut, as elsewhere, to pitiful levels. At Rottingdean, the landowning family, the Beards were motivated by the religious beliefs of Quakerism, something for which the local labourers had cause to be grateful. Elsewhere, landowners could not or would not sustain men on a living wage. During the eighteenth century, new methods of agriculture re-vitalised the old market towns, Chichester and Lewes in particular enjoyed a renaissance at this time. The wealth of these towns remained confined to a few, whose prosperity manifested itself in the re-building or 're-fronting' of many timber-framed houses in the new, classical style.

Religious decline was very apparent in eighteenth century Sussex, and was only checked by the rise of Methodism. The religious fervour of the sixteenth and seventeenth centuries had given way to indifference. All across the county, parish churches fell into decay, even complete dilapidation. The parish church of St. James the Less at North Lancing was a case in point. The roof collapsed, and birds were nesting in the ruins. At Heene the chapel was neglected, and the last sermon was given by a mad lawyer, whose incoherent rantings attracted an unruly and ribald crowd. At near-by Durrington the church fell down, and the villagers were told to worship at West Tarring instead. This is not to say that atheism had become rampant, on the contrary, people still professed to Christian beliefs, it was simply that the old fervour had gone.

Hove Church Sussex, sadly dilapidated in 1850 (WSCC)

Drunkenness

Herbert Morley and his puritan brethren would have been horrified to observe how the Spirit of God had been substituted by the spirit of the bottle. It would be very hard to exaggerate the everyday drunkenness of life in Georgian Sussex. People of all classes got drunk all the time; they were often sorry for it afterwards, both physically and spiritually, but that did not stop them from getting drunk again, whenever the opportunity presented itself. For a glimpse into this world, we can do no better than read the diaries of Thomas Turner of East Hoathly, which span the years 1754-1765. Turner was a shop-keeper; he was also at various times, the village schoolmaster, tax-collector, churchwarden and undertaker. His diaries record the drunken predilections of his neighbours, and his own forlorn attempts to curb his own consumption. It was not unusual to find the residents of East Hoathly suffering the effects of alcohol at all times of the day. The following extract, from February 1758, records a night of debauchery, in which the parson and his wife appear to have been the chief instigators. I quote Turner in full, so that the reader can appreciate in full the sordid scene he describes, as well as his own doubts and anxieties regarding such behaviour -

"After supper our behaviour was far from serious, harmless, mirth for it was downright obstreperous mirth mixed with a great deal of folly and stupidity. Our diversion was dancing (or jumping about) without a violin or any music, singing of foolish and bawdy healths and more such-like stupidity, and drinking all the time as fast as could be well poured down; and the parson of the parish was one amongst the mixed multitude all the time, so doubtless in point of sound divinity it was all harmless. But if conscience dictates right from wrong, as doubtless it sometimes does, mine is one that we may say is soon offended. For I must say I am always very uneasy at such behaviour, thinking it is not like the behaviour of the primitive Christians, which I imagine was most in conformity to our Saviour's gospel. Nor would I on the other hand be thought to be either a cynic or a stoic, but let social improving discourse pass around the company. But, however, about 3.30[am], finding myself to have as much liquor as would do me good, I slipped away unobserved, leaving my wife to make my excuse; for sure it was rude, but ill-manners are preferable to drunkenness (though I was very far from being sober). However, I came home, thank God, very safe and well without ever tumbling or any other misfortune, and Mr. French brought my wife home about 5.10[am]."

Turner's ordeal was not over yet, less than an hour later, he was awakened by the arrival of Mr. Porter, the parson, his wife, and other revellers -

" This morn about 6 o'clock, just as my wife was gladly got into bed and had laid herself down to rest, we was awakened by Mrs. Porter, who pretended she wanted some cream of tartar. But as soon as my wife got out of bed, she vowed she should come down, which she complied with and found she, Mr. Porter,

Mr. Fuller and his wife with a lighted candle, part of a bottle of wine and a glass. Then the next thing in course must be to have me downstairs, which I being apprized of, fastened my door. But, however, upstairs they came and threatened and also attempted to break open my door, which I found they would do; so I therefore ordered the boys to open it. But as soon as ever it was open, they poured into my room, and as modesty forbid me to get out of bed in the presence of women, so I refrained. But their immodesty permitted them to draw me out of bed (as the common phrase is) tipsy turvey. But, however, at the intercession of Mr. Porter they permitted me to put on my breeches (as it was no more than to cast a veil over what undoubtedly they had before that time discovered); as also, instead of my clothes, they gave me time to put on my wife's petticoat. In this manner they made me dance with them without shoes or stockings until they had emptied their bottle of wine and also a bottle of my beer..."

There we must leave Turner, dancing in his wife's petticoat, to the drunken amusement of the parson and his other 'guests'. The entry in the diary for the next day, simply records, "Sadly indisposed." Such scenes were not unique to East Hoathly, and were surely repeated in villages all across Sussex at that time.

The drunkenness of the age was only matched by its violence. On Ditchling Common to this day there stands a solitary wooden post. Many strangers are baffled as to its significance. It is known as Jacob's Post, and it marks the spot where in 1734, a notorious robber and murderer Jacob Harris was gibbeted. Gibbeting involved the body of an executed felon being hung in chains from a high pole, and there left to moulder and rot - a ghastly warning, it was hoped, to those tempted by a life of crime.

Jacob Harris had been a member of a gang of thieves who had broken into an alehouse on Ditchling Common. The landlord had been seized in the stables, and his throat cut, "from ear to ear". Once inside the premises the robbers had inadvertently woken the maid, who came downstairs to investigate. She too was killed. Harris then went upstairs, where he found the landlord's wife, ill in bed. He dragged her from the bed, and cut her throat. While it would be wrong to say such outrages were common, neither would it be correct to say they were unique. The murders committed by the Hawkhurst Gang of smugglers in the following decade were equally brutal.

Smuggling

Smuggling still fascinates the modern mind. Pubs and cottages, caves and coves, supposedly associated with smuggling abound throughout southern England. This writer is frequently asked to speak to local societies and associations on the topic of smuggling. Indeed it is by far and away the most requested topic. A veil of romantic delusion has been cast over this desperate period in Sussex history. For, despite the swashbuckling image, smuggling was the product of harsh economic conditions, and for many people represented the

Smugglers prepare to bury a victim (WSCC)

only viable escape from a life of poverty. In the Weald in particular, the decline of so many local industries created high unemployment, and the jobs that remained were poorly paid. Even the old rights over common land were being eroded by the ongoing march of parliamentary enclosure.

The Duke of Newcastle's enclosure of Ashdown Forest effectively 'privatised' the land. Fences were erected, and the local population were told to keep out. No longer would they be able to gather firewood from the forest, nor graze their animals within its confines. To the Duke, Ashdown Forest was a derelict wasteland that could, with private investment, be turned into a highly productive area. It needed management, and the introduction of modern methods of farming and forestry. In some respects the Acts of Enclosure passed by Parliament during the eighteenth and early nineteenth century, had effects not dissimilar to the great land grab that followed the Reformation. It can be argued that the process was in the long term interests of the rural economy. What can not be disputed is that the enclosure of Ashdown Forest was certainly not in the short-term interests of the local population. Correspondence of the Duke's steward, Abraham Baley, has survived, and show the lengths he went to in order to keep the local people out of the forest. On 31 January 1763, he wrote -

"I have a list of about ten poor wretches chiefly women and children that have been pilfering the woods this cold weather and intend having them all before a magistrate at the first proper opportunity and if I can prevail upon the justices to act as they ought shall get several of them whipped, the one man sent to the house of correction but I don't know that anything will be sufficient to keep them honest. They are a parcel of the most distressed and miserable objects I ever saw among the human species."

Despite his efforts the 'pilfering' continued, forcing Baley to take even more drastic action. On 13 May, he obtained an order to pull down the cottage of one of the transgressors. Such action created bitterness. As recently as 1881, one commentator observed, "They are a wild tribe, these foresters, and education and civilisation are making slow inroads upon their uncultured manners and love of independence. Time was, when they were a really dangerous crew to deal with, and the wide sweep of country covering Ashdown Forest was a domain in which the Queen's writs could scarcely be said to run."

In other parts of the eastern Weald a legacy of lawless times was still recalled. Writing in 1870, the Sussex antiquarian M.A.Lower, wrote of the "uncivilised condition" of Crowborough in the previous century, and how Crowborough Warren had been "a favourite resort for smugglers from the coast." Writing about the same time, Charles Francis Trower of Burwash, remembered how his parish had known violent and lawless days -

"Men now living, or their fathers, can remember how it was scarcely safe to ride after nightfall over Burwash Downs, and how often the inmates of lone farm-houses were scared by the assaults of burglars. The parish seems to have had an unenviable notoriety for being the birthplace or sheltering place of rick-burners, sheep-stealers, and thieves. The immediate ancestors of those, who now pursue a quiet and honest life of husbandry, gained an illicit profit, and led dissolute lives, in conveying kegs of brandy up the country with relays of horses from the sea-coast."

Both Lower and Trower remind us that although smuggled goods were brought ashore, as needs must, on the coast, they were quickly transported into the smugglers' country of the High Weald. The other district, just outside the county, with a similar reputation, was Romney Marsh, and once again poverty and a want of gainful employment contributed to the

Execise man, William Galley is lowered into his grave (WSCC)

rise of smuggling. Not until the creation of the Coastguard service in 1822, followed by the East Sussex Constabulary of Police in 1838, did travellers dare to pass through such country unarmed.

The high duties imposed on luxury imports, such as tea, spirits and tobacco, ensured that smuggling was a lucrative business. At no time did the trade in contraband seriously decline during these years, although two decades do stand out as having been especially violent: the 1740's and the 1820's. The latter can be explained by the acute economic conditions of the period, and the former by the activities of the Hawkhurst Gang - the most powerful and the most violent of all the smuggling organisations that ever operated in the county.

Hawkhurst is actually situated just over the Sussex border in Kent, but most of the gang's activities took place in Sussex. By the early 1740's the leader of the organisation, Arthur Gray, had become so wealthy that he was living in splendour in a mansion on Seacox Heath. His men extorted money from the near-by villages, and swaggered around the district in the manner of feudal lords. Much of the gang's history reads more like fiction than historical fact. The incredible story of how the villagers of Goudhurst formed themselves into a militia to defend their parish against the smugglers is the most remarkable story of all, and reads more like a script for a Hollywood film than an episode of real local history. Yet the events can be verified, including the gunfight around the church in which George Kingsmill, one of the leading smugglers, was shot off his horse and killed. The King's writ no more extended over the parishes of the Sussex/ Kent border than it did over the rebellious colonists in America.

The Hawkhurst smugglers acted with impunity. They ambushed and murdered Thomas Carswell, a Customs and Excise official. They stormed the Customs House at Poole and retrieved contraband tea, previously seized by Naval vessels in the Channel. They fought and killed soldiers, including Royal Dragoons at various places along the Sussex coast. They tortured an informer and then buried him alive. They treated a captured Customs officer in a similar manner, then threw him down a disused well. When he was heard still to be groaning, they hurled boulders of flint down the well, until he moaned no more. Most notoriously of all, they brutally kicked and whipped to death Richard Hawkins, a thirteen year old boy from Slindon, whom they wrongly accused of stealing a

Richard Hawkins is whipped to death
(WSCC)

sack of tea. Excessive drinking was associated with most of these outrages. Two hundred and fifty years later, many places in Sussex still recall the deeds of this gang. Even in the sleepy suburb of Goring, near Worthing, we find a quiet residential road named 'Smuggler's Walk'; not far from here the smugglers fought a battle with Royal Dragoons, in which one of the dragoons was killed. Only the Jacobites posed a greater threat to the English State than these smugglers, who appeared invulnerable to all attempts to break their hold over the county.

When, in 1749, the gang was finally broken, a great 'show trial' was held at the guildhall at Chichester. The senior Assize judges, who normally came no further south into Sussex than Horsham, fearing for their safety if they did, presided over the proceedings. All the defendants were found guilty, and hanged together on the Broyle, north of the city, in the largest mass execution in the county's history. Later their bodies were gibbeted around the county, at the scenes of their most notorious crimes. A plaque still recalls the trial and executions. Yet despite the hopes of the Duke of Richmond, who had done more than anyone else in Sussex to bring these men to justice, smuggling was not broken. Poverty and the prospect of rich rewards, continued to entice new recruits into the smuggling game, although none ever repeated the success, or the violence of the Hawkhurst Gang.

One of the most elusive and colourful figures in the Sussex smuggling story was John Olliver, miller of Highdown Hill. Despite the outward appearance of respectability, Olliver was almost certainly an important person in the 'free trade' business. It is even said that his windmill was used to signal to smuggling vessels in the Channel (it is doubtful if any mill in the county was as visible from the sea as the Highdown Mill). His small cottage on the eastern slopes of Highdown was surmounted by a weather vane, which depicted a smuggler being pursued by an Excise officer with a drawn cutlass, who in his turn was being chased by a old woman with a raised broom. Olliver gained permission from the local landowner, Westbrooke Richardson, to construct his own tomb on Highdown, which stood for some forty years before Olliver's actual death at the age of eighty-four in 1793. He also kept his coffin under his bed, and wrote poetry, contemplating death. Two thousand people attended his funeral (the entire local population at that time), who were provided with food and drink. The 'wake' ended in a drunken riot. In his will, Olliver left several substantial properties, including the Hollies in Tarring High Street, a building which survives till the present day. Despite his own frugal lifestyle, he had clearly amassed a great deal of wealth over the years, and judging from the turnout for his funeral, brought a great deal of wealth into the district.

Robert Bignell was another smuggler who became famous in his own lifetime, and whose deeds were recalled for years to come, although not necessarily with affection. He was born at Clayton, and was involved in crime for all his adult life. As well as being a smuggler he was also a known poacher, burglar, footpad and murderer. In 1802 it appeared his criminal career was over, when he was detained by officers of the Customs and Excise. However instead of the gallows, he was offered the opportunity of saving his neck, by entering the employ of the Excise, as a 'special' officer. Bignell accepted the chance for life, and took the commission.

On 30 November in the same year, Bignell killed the 'Great Jack Webber', a well-known smuggler in mid Sussex. In front of many witnesses, Bignell shot Webber dead at the inn on St. John's Common. He was later arrested and charged with murder, but after a glowing testimonial from the Customs and Excise, he was acquitted. Bignell, still in official employ, moved to Bristol in 1803, the smuggling capital of the west country. Instead of repeating his 'success' in Sussex, Bignell absconded with £120.

Three years later, Bignell was back in Sussex, where he was identified following an aggravated burglary at Albourne. He was later recognised by the landlord of the White Hart at Ditchling, who wrestled him to the ground, and with the help of some of his customers, conveyed him to the House of Correction at Lewes. Once again Bignell nearly cheated justice: a rope ladder was smuggled into the gaol by a sympathiser. Whilst scaling the outside wall, Bignell was seized by cramp, and fell back into the prison yard - his luck had finally run out. He was hanged at Horsham in March 1807, in front of a crowd of 3,000. On the gallows he made a speech, declaring the day to be the happiest of his life, and concluded by reading some of his own poetry. The execution was so momentous, that many years later, old men, trying to recall past events would describe them as being "so many summers" before or after "they hanged Bignell."

A whole book could easily be written, chronicling the deeds of Georgian criminals in Sussex. Mention can briefly be made of John Breads, who in attempting to murder the mayor of Rye, mistakenly killed his cousin, the deputy mayor. Or James Petitt of Jevington, whose career so closely mirrored that of Bignell. On seven occasions between 1790 and 1799, Petitt appeared in court on a capital charge, on six occasions he got off. He was finally convicted and sentenced to death for horse-stealing, but the sentence was subsequently commuted to transportation to Australia. In Sussex, between 1650 and 1800, 431 people were sentenced to death, of whom about half were respited, most like Petitt, being transported. For the thirty years 1800-1830 alone, 300 people were sentenced to death by Sussex courts, although only thirty-six of these were carried out. It is a sobering thought that more people were executed in Sussex in those years than in the whole of either Germany or France.

Sussex can boast, if that is the appropriate word, to have carried out the last executions in the country by pressing and by fire. In 1735, John Weekes was sentenced to 'Peine forte et dure', that is to be pressed to death. His crime was that he had refused to make a plea at his trial for another offence. He was pinned to the ground, and a wooden board placed over his body, onto which successively heavy weights were added. After all the weights had been placed on Weekes, he was observed still to be breathing, at which point the executioner jumped on top, and finished the job.

In 1776, the last sentence for 'Petit Treason', the murder of a husband by his wife, was carried out. As ordained by law, Ann Cruttenden was dragged to the place of execution on a hurdle, and there tied to a pole, around which a fire was kindled. Before the flames reached her, she was strangled by a long rope around her neck. Twenty-four years earlier another husband killer, Ann Whale was similarly executed. Her cousin, Sarah Pledge had conspired in the murder, but not being the wife of the victim, she was hanged in the ordinary fashion. A witness to the macabre events on Horsham Common, described the scene -

"The parson prayed for and with her for upwards of half an hour before she was strangled; this was about five minutes before the fire was kindled, which was one of the greatest ever known upon such a melancholy occasion. There were upwards of three hundred and one half of faggots and three loads of cord wood so that it must have continued burning till Saturday night or Sunday morning. The faggots eclipsed the sight of her for some time, but in about five minutes the violence of the flames consumed a part thereof which falling away gave the spectators an opportunity of seeing her - a very affecting and disagreeable object, for she was all consumed to a skeleton. She said nothing at the place of execution - the whole ceremony was carried out with the strictest decorum and decency and there was the biggest concourse of people ever known on a like occasion - the body of Sarah Pledge was put into a tallow chandlers hamper and carried to Doctor Dennet Junior, of Storrington, to be dissected agreeable to the late Act of Parliament."

Were such events to happen today in a Third World country, we would be appalled, yet not so long ago it was happening here, and being regarded as conforming to standards of "decorum and decency" no less! Sarah Pledge's body was sent for dissection; this was not unusual, and was sometimes performed in public. Richard Grazemark, the Ferring axe-murderer of 1793, was dissected after execution. His skin was removed and sent to a tannery, from which leather pouches were made. These mementous were much sought after by the public.

William Albery, the great Horsham historian, and the first person to detail the criminal history of Sussex, was not unmoved by the brutal qualities of eighteenth and early nineteenth century justice, of which he commented - "The catalogue of crimes and punishments during this long time can be read by the curious, pondered by the thoughtful, and lamented by the humane." Albery also realised that crime was very much related to class. Writing of the execution of thirteen year old Richard Bridger, sentenced to death for stealing £100 at Chichester, Alberry wrote, "By a similar financial action done smartly and on a much larger scale he might have secured a Knighthood and a marble monument, instead of the attentions of the hangman."

The Swing Riots

On 5 November 1830, riots broke out at Brede in East Sussex, which were to spread across the entire county. Kent had already seen violence, and over the next month the much of southern England was engulfed in an orgy of arson, machine-breaking and riot. The trouble was ostensibly caused by the introduction of the threshing machine, which did away with the need to thresh corn by hand with flails, thereby depriving men of work at the very time they needed it most, with winter approaching. There was however more at work in the minds of the people than resentment towards new technology. For many years the pay and conditions of the rural workforce had been declining. Where once a man could have expected to be employed for life, now he was lucky if he could secure employment for a year, and many labourers were reduced to piece work. Any status and pride the peasant might once have enjoyed was fast becoming a distant memory. The loss of common land due to enclosure hastened the

'The Skeleton at the Plough' – a contemporary cartoon

demise of the old peasant class, and led to an increase in the number of men entirely dependent on wages for their survival.

Smuggling had once offered an illicit income, but times were getting harder for the 'free traders'. Following the end of the Napoleonic wars in 1815, Admiral Joseph McCulloch, known to his men for obvious reasons as "Flogging Joey" was granted permission by the government to establish a naval blockade in the Channel, to intercept smuggling vessels. He hand-picked men from the ranks to serve in this new force, which was armed, highly motivated, and comparatively well paid, something the Excise service had never been. So great were McCulloch's successes in frustrating the efforts of the smugglers, that in 1822 his force became a permanent feature, to be known as the Coastguard. It is interesting to recall, therefore, that our modern day Coastguard began life as a paramilitary force, charged with the suppression of smuggling.

Throughout the 1820's vicious skirmishes took place between the smugglers and the Coastguard, with fatalities on both sides. The arrest and conviction in 1826 of George Ransley and several other members of the Aldington Gang was the high point of McCulloch's career, for the 'Roaring Ransleys' were the most formidable smuggling operation in the south, benefiting from their own firm of solicitors, and a private doctor!

Some years later a gang operating in West Sussex, led by a thirty-one year old stonemason, William Cowerson, was led into a trap at Worthing by the Coastguard. In the battle that followed, Cowerson was killed. His funeral at Steyning attracted large crowds, and an elaborate tombstone (which can still be found in the churchyard) was erected. These set-backs for the smugglers were serious, and added to the growing swell of discontent and anger in the countryside. More and more men were falling on 'parish relief', the social security of those days. The system was not national, but based on parishes. In some parishes most of the adult male population were claiming some form of relief, this in turn caused a massive increase in the poor rates. While the aristocratic families could afford these ever increasing taxes, the smaller farmers and village tradesmen could not and many fell into debt and even bankruptcy.

A West Sussex gentleman, wrote of the distress in the Horsham district -

"At a bench of Magistrates held here on Saturday the Bench room was crowded with distressed labourers from the surrounding parishes, but more especially from the Parish of Rudgwick, who represented their deplorable case to the Magistrates. They asserted that the whole of their allowance amounted to no more than 3s 0d per week for working on the roads, that out of this sum they had to pay 1s 6d for lodging, 6d for washing and mending, that the remaining 1s 0d was spent at a rate of 2d per day on food, that the 2d was divided for two meals per day being 1d for each meal, and this was the whole of their subsistence! The Magistrates heard this distressing account but the men were dismissed without any relief. Such is the desperate condition to which the labourers in the surrounding parishes are reduced. Where it will all end God only knows, but if something be not done soon all will be confusion and bankruptcy for the above system of payment is becoming universal, the farmers being unable to hire labourers oppressed as they are with tithes and taxes."

The '10%' tax or 'tithe' to the Church was resented by just about everyone. Many of the clergy in Sussex were accused of being idle, even to the extent of failing to be present to conduct Sunday services. The disdain in which the clergy were held at this time took many years to subside. Writing in 1888, the Rev. Cocker-Egerton of Burwash, remembered a labourer shouting out to him one election day, "more fat pigs, less fat parsons!" It is to be wondered if there has ever been a period in Sussex history when feelings of discontent and resentment were so widespread. The disturbances of 1830 began at Brede, a place long associated with protest and dissent.

In the days leading up to 5 November, there were increasing reports of fires, and attacks on property, at Battle, Hartfield and Icklesham. The eastern corner of East Sussex was the focus for so many grievances, and at Brede they first found their collective expression. The labourers of the parish banded together, and by sheer weight of numbers, forced the local farmers to meet them at the Red Lion Inn. The labourers demanded that wages be raised to 2s 3d per day, with immediate effect, and then to 2s 6d per day from 1 March the following year. A man with three children should receive an extra 1s 3d per week, and an incremental increase for each extra child. Lastly, they demanded that Mr. Abel, the Overseer of the Poor, be removed "out of the parish to any adjoining parish and to use him with civility." All the demands were conceded. Mr. Abel, the overbearing taskmaster of those on poor relief, was wheeled out of Brede in the parish cart by a jubilant crowd, and dumped at the parish boundary.

Within days similar scenes were witnessed at Burwash, Ticehurst, Fairlight, Warbleton, Mayfield and Heathfield. At Ninefield it was noticed that prominent in the crowd were smugglers, armed with pistols. There being no professional police force in the county, the magistrates were reliant on the farmers agreeing to be sworn in as Special Constables, but many farmers refused, others simply made themselves unavailable. Unable to fulfil their duty to keep the peace, magistrates frequently advised farmers to agree to the labourers' terms, as the best way of preserving order. The farmers of Dallington, wrote in despairing terms to the Home Secretary, pleading for assistance -

"We the undersigned farmers, tradesmen and others, rate-payers in the small agricultural parish of Dallington in the County of Sussex, consider it our duty to make known to His Majesty and the Government through, the Secretary of the Home Department, that altho' unable to bear it we have met the wishes of the magistrates of this district by raising the wages of the labourers and the relief of the paupers on a scale which we positively cannot continue for any length of time without bringing us all to one common ruin, and which we have done to prevent our property from being destroyed by incendiaries. We therefore implore His Majesty's Government, if they value the existence of the Middle Class of society, to take off all taxes which press on the industrious classes, otherwise there will be but two classes, the one most miserably poor and the other most extremely rich."

By 15 November the trouble had spread to West Sussex. Mobs assembled at Bosham and Bognor. At Lancing the Riot Act was read. At Worthing the Rector's tithe feast was disrupted by a belligerent crowd, demanding that the tithes be suspended. Across the county landowners and magistrates received threatening letters, one of which warned, "Revenge for thee is on the wing, from thy determined Captain Swing." With the mythical 'Swing' as their general, the labourers realised the potential they had to effect change. At Horsham, described as being "a hot-bed of sedition", mobs assembled at the Carfax, as witnessed by John Browne, a town constable -

"As the church clock struck three, a party with a flag made of two handkerchiefs hoisted upon an ash twig, about fifteen feet long appeared coming up West Street: at this moment another party came in from the East and another from the North, and having congratulated each other with a moderate hurrah they proceeded quietly to the church...."

Just as at Brede and elsewhere, the labourers forced the wealthier farmers and landowners, including Sir Timothy Shelley of Field Place, to accompany them. The meeting was stormy and menacing, one of the labourers leaders threatened to set fire to the church, "with the gentlemen in it" if their demands were not met. One of those to whom the threat was directed never doubted it was made in earnest, and many years later he recalled, "I am sorry to say that whilst life remains with me the terror of that time will never be obliterated from my memory..."

Whilst there seemed no power able to respond to the riots in East Sussex, in the west of the county the old aristocratic families quickly took up the challenge to restore order in the countryside. The Duke of Richmond enrolled a militia of farmers, shopkeepers and 'respectable' labourers, whom he efficiently organised into sections and districts, with local commanders. By such methods were the disturbances quelled in the west. Several hundred labourers were arrested. The Duke of Wellington approved of such tactics, commenting, "it is astonishing how soon the country was tranquillised, and that in the best way by the activity and spirit of the gentlemen." At the Quarter Sessions held at Horsham in January 1831, there were the largest number of defendants ever recorded. Instead of sitting the usual one day, or at most two, these sessions lasted an unprecedented four days.

It has to be said that the West Sussex magistrates showed greater leniency than their counter-parts in other counties, where hundreds of men were transported to Australia, and several were executed. In West Sussex a total of twenty-seven men were transported, and one, convicted of the capital charge of arson, was sentenced to death. Edmund Bushby had set fire to a hay-rick at East Preston. Death seemed an extreme punishment for a crime which neither threatened life, nor endangered buildings. Mr. Santuary, a Horsham magistrate, and High Sheriff of the county, rode to Brighton to see the King. Santuary hoped to persuade the King to use his Royal Prerogative to commute Bushby's sentence to one of transportation. The King was adamant however; his view, shared by those now in government was that harsh measures were needed in order to restore order, and clemency would be sending the wrong message. So Bushby was hanged outside Horsham gaol, in front of a large but sombre crowd.

In the eastern part of the county, further executions followed for arson: Thomas Bufford, December 1831; Samuel Thorncraft, April 1832; George Wren, January 1833; and William Goodsell, January 1834. Bufford, who came from Alfriston was a known smuggler. He displayed a steely courage on the gallows, rolling up his sleeves and loosening his collar as the hangman approached. George Wren of Uckfield presented a pitiful spectacle. He was only nineteen years of age and had been born in the workhouse. A boot print found near the smouldering rick was said to be his, and his claims that he had tried to put the fire out were dismissed. Wren was no radical, nor orator, but as he stood on the gallows, with the crowds gathered around him, he managed to summon up the words to clearly express both the injustice and the barbarism of his sentence - "Good people, I am brought to this scaffold to be murdered for a thing I know nothing of. I am brought like a bullock to the slaughter, I am brought to this end by false swearing and now stand before the awful throne of God who knows all secrets."

With arson endemic in the countryside, someone had to pay the price, and who better than a hardened smuggler or an illegitimate son of the workhouse? Faced with such a serious break-down in law and order, the East Sussex magistrates were some of the first in the country to implement the 1838 Police Act, which made provision for the creation of professional police forces, funded from the rates. In the west of the county, the Act was not welcomed. Here the old aristocratic landowners saw law and order as their domain, the last thing they wanted to see was some new policing body outside of their direct control. The middle class were not keen, they after all would have to pay for it through higher rates, and the labouring classes, increasingly dependent as they were on poaching and other illegal activities certainly had no reason to be enthusiastic.

Nineteen years later, all but a handful of the English counties had implemented the 1838 Act. One of the exceptions was West Sussex. A second Act of 1857 compelled counties like West Sussex to create county constabularies. The county magistrates carried out their obligations with little enthusiasm. The first West Sussex force was of the minimum size allowed by the Act, and the first constables were even required to buy their own uniforms! As the years went by the hostility softened, but suspicion and scepticism remained. As late as 1870, it was not uncommon to find middle class residents complaining about the cost, and the conduct of the new police. One group of Westbourne residents wrote a letter to the West Sussex Gazette, raising their concerns-

"Of what real service are the rural police? Within two or three years there have been in this immediate neighbourhood two or three cases of fowl stealing, as many of sheep stealing, in not one instance of which have the police been able to trace the delinquent! While, however, their institution has effected a great increase in the burden of the... rates, their real utility may be considered as bounded by their activity in rummaging the contents of honest men's carts; summonsing persons where cattle may have strayed into a lane, and laborers tired and foot sore for riding without reins, as well as dressing in plain clothes and asking for drink at public houses on Sunday during forbidden hours."

On 5 November in particular, the rowdy scenes typical of traditional Bonfire Night celebrations in Sussex attracted the attentions of the police, who tried to curtail and suppress these riotous proceedings. Today most people would only be too pleased to know that the police had intervened to stop men and youths rolling blazing barrels through the streets, and even on occasions, burning boats. They would applaud police efforts to arrest those guilty of throwing stones and fireworks. Yet in Victorian Sussex there were many people of high social standing, including even magistrates, who regarded such behaviour as traditional, and demonstrative of local patriotism. Even when serious rioting took place, there were those ever ready to blame the police, accusing them of "interfering" and "provoking" the disturbances. On one occasion at Worthing, when the rioters attacked the police, the magistrates refused to read the Riot Act.

It is hard today to realise how close-knit the small towns and villages of Sussex were little more than a century ago, and how much outside influences were resented. This is perhaps most graphically illustrated by the riots that took place all over Sussex between in 1883 and 1891, directed against the Salvation Army. This evangelical movement from London, with its militant posture and its disregard for social norms (e.g. allowing women equal status with men), enraged conservative opinion in Sussex. At Worthing in 1884, the disturbances were so serious that the army had to be brought in to restore order on the streets. At Eastbourne in 1891, the rioters were actually inspired and encouraged by the mayor. Yet these were the last indignant blasts of the old order. The new roads, and especially the railways, were transforming Sussex. More and more outsiders were moving into the county. The towns were growing at the expense of the countryside. The Education Acts of 1870 onwards imbued new ideas and attitudes into the minds of the young. It was not however until after the First World War that the prosperous, largely crime-free Sussex we know today fully emerged, the product of a massive influx into the county of commuters and the retired. Everything has its price. In Sussex, the price for prosperity and order in the streets was paid for by the loss of the county identity. Many of those who welcomed the decline of drunkenness and rioting, also lamented the passing of the old traditions, the old rural smock, and the rich southern dialects.

Routing a Salvation Army procession

HASTINGS, RYE & DISTRICT

Hastings and Rye and the surrounding district stand apart from the rest of Sussex, and not simply because they are to be found at the far east of the county. The landscape here is more wild and far less tamed than elsewhere in Sussex. Rugged sandstone cliffs loom over Hastings, and there is a complete absence of the chalk and flint which are so abundant elsewhere on the Sussex coast. Whereas most of the county's coastline has been, and is being eroded by the sea, east of Hastings the land mass is actually increasing. Winchelsea and Rye, which were once thriving ports are now over a mile inland. But the differences are more than geological. The people of this district were always considered a race apart and even had their own distinct dialect, which was quite different from that found in the rest of Sussex or in Kent. In Saxon times this area was dominated by a tribe called the Haestingas, which appears to have existed outside the control of either the Jutes of Kent or the Saxons of Sussex. After the Norman Conquest and the famous Battle of Hastings (see p29), the new rulers perpetuated the old division in the 'Rape of Hastings', which was controlled from Hastings Castle by Robert de Eu. In medieval times Rye became one of the famous Cinque Ports, and had virtual autonomy. Not until 1889 was the old town truly integrated into the county of East Sussex. Although many residents and local businessmen today complain about the poor state of the roads in this part of Sussex, and in particular the lack of by-passes, it is this very absence of modern infrastructure which enables this part of the county to retain something of its old identity.

Hastings

Hastings has proved to be the great survivor of Sussex. It has remained an important town throughout history, when others have succumbed to changing circumstances and become sleepy backwaters. Most significantly it survived the ravages of Duke William's men in 1066, and went on to become an important medieval port. Then again in the nineteenth century, when many old towns were displaced by new resort towns on the coast, or commuter towns along the new railways, Hastings adapted to change. By the end of the nineteenth century, a new 'seaside' Hastings had emerged, along with the new suburb of St. Leonards. The population more than doubled in twenty years, from 11,789 in 1841 to 26,631 in 1861. In the next twenty years this rate of growth was outpaced by Eastbourne, but Hastings was not sidelined, and continued to attract both visitors and new residents. Yet despite all this change, the Old Town remained true to itself, and even today it retains a very special character, not duplicated in other towns.

Hastings' success at reconstructing itself in a modern guise was all the more remarkable given its reputation as a lawless place, where respectable persons had to tread with care. The area of All Saints Street was especially renowned.

You will find the graves of smugglers in All Saints churchyard. Even at the end of the nineteenth century the legacy of those days was not forgotten, as Augustus Hare noted -

"The street is now chiefly inhabited by the Hastings fisherfolk, who lead a life apart and intermarry. The name 'Chopback' infuriates them. Hastings pirates used to torture their captives in that way, and even in the middle of the last century [the eighteenth] 'Ruxley's crew' were hanged for torturing the master of a Dutch brig to death by chopping down the ribs from the spine."

Hare's contention that this was "a cruelty handed down from Danish times" cannot be verified, although it certainly bears a similarity to the Viking torture and execution of 'blood red eagle'. The influence of the fishing fraternity appears to have been the chief obstacle to Hastings' progress, as this extract from a letter written to the London Chronicle in 1760 suggests -

" The situation of Hastings itself is as bad as any place that stands in a hole can be; and there is a great addition of badness by the proximity of the sea, which comes close up to the lowest houses, and is abundantly dulcified by the stinking guts of the fish, plentifully spread all over the town, and the lovely and alluring sight of drying dabbs at every house, which indeed, is the chief food and support of the inhabitants."

Over 120 years later, Richard Jefferies was no more impressed. He thought the Western Road at Brighton bad enough for smells in the summer months, "But [it] is sweet indeed," he tells us, "compared to Hastings which in hot weather stenches everywhere, like a leather dresser's in Bermondsey, yea, worse, like old boots. If Brighton sins, Hastings sins seven times seven."

Not everyone was so critical. E V Lucas, who did not especially like seaside towns, certainly thought Hastings preferable to Brighton -

"Hastings has two advantages over both Brighton and Eastbourne: it can produce a genuine piece of antiquity, and seen from the sea it has a picturesque quality that neither of those towns possesses. Indeed under certain conditions of light, Hastings is magnificent, with the craggy Castle Hill in its midst surmounted by its imposing ruin. The smoke of the town, rising and spreading, shrouds the modernity of the sea front, and the castle on its commanding height seems to be brooding over the shores of old romance."

The writer of an article published in the fashionable journal, 'Black and White' in 1891 even had a good word to say for the much maligned residents of the Old Town -

" The inhabitants of the old part of Hastings are in many respects a race apart. They claim a long line of antiquity for many of their leading families, and their quaint dialect, their tan frocks, and the fact that they are all fishermen, seems to stamp them as the direct descendants of the indigenous inhabitants. It is very amusing to enter into conversation with some of these old, bluff, weather-beaten salts, who have passed all their lives on the Channel or in the

Fisherman at Hastings in the 1850's (WSCC)

ingle nooks of their strange picturesque shanties. They are a proud people these fisher-folk, and in spite of their apparent indigence have in many instances amassed large sums, as is clearly shown by the fact that some of them own two, or even three, large fishing smacks, each of which cost between £600 and £800 to build."

The tall huts used by the fishermen to dry their nets can still be seen at Hastings. A museum dedicated to the history of the fishing community is located close by and contains many interesting items associated with the fishermen and their way of life.

If the Hastings people were a hardy lot it was due in part to their proximity to France, from where raids against the East Sussex coast were frequently undertaken. On several occasions Hastings was attacked, the last time being as recently as 1796. A French raid in 1691 left two cannon balls lodged in the tower of St. Clement's Church, which remain there to this day. John Collier, mayor of Hastings in the mid eighteenth century needed to keep a sharp look out for local smuggling gangs as well as the French. His position was more akin to that of a 'Wild West' Marshall rather than that of a civic dignitary. In the same comparative vein it could also be said that Collier resembled the corrupt American mayors of the mid-twentieth century, whose allegiance was to the highest bidder. Collier was very much the Duke of Newcastle's man. As stated elsewhere in this book Thomas Pelham, Duke of Newcastle, was one of the most powerful men in England, and his family had retained a controlling interest in the life of East Sussex for generations. However the Duke found it much harder to exert his influence over the unruly people who lived in and around Hastings. In Collier he found just the man to look after his interests. The Duke 'looked after' Collier, and Collier served his master well. The son of a town publican, Collier ended his days in a fine house in Hastings High Street, today known as Old Hastings House. Yet even the wealthy and powerful were not shielded from misery and suffering: Collier fathered twenty children, all of whom died young.

Through a mixture of threats, inducements and appeasement, Collier created a semblance of order in Hastings. But after his death in 1760, Hastings returned to its old ways, as the following newspaper article for 1768 demonstrates -

"They write from Hastings in Sussex, that a very tumultuous mob rose there by beat of drum, and insisted upon having wheat at 5s per bushel. They then went to the house of Mr. White, a farmer in that neighbourhood, dragged him out to the middle of one of his own fields, forced him to stay there while they broke open his granary and destroyed all his wheat; after this they returned and paraded it about town. The Mayor being afraid to oppose them, John Nicoll, Esq; a Justice of the Peace, caused the ringleader to be brought before him, and charged an officer... to convey him to Horsham gaol; but the mob soon rescued their captain, and then proceeded in a most riotous manner to Mr. Nicoll's house, whom they probably would have killed, if he had not made his escape through the back door."

Rough seas batter Hastings old Town in 1875 (WSCC)

Even as late as the 1870's, we find law and order still a problem in the town. It was said that policemen dared not 'box the ears' of local delinquents, for fear of the consequences. Vandalism was rife, and letters were written to the local newspapers, •complaining of the gangs of youths who fought each other in the streets. For many years Hastings continued with old methods of punishment which other towns had long since abandoned. For instance, the stocks were still in use in 1839, when Thomas Sadler was locked in them for four hours, having committed a violent assault upon the landlord of the King's Head. In 1872, in an attempt to attract better recruits to the local police force, pay for constables was raised by 25%, and their holiday entitlement increased from five days a year to twelve.

The Parade, Hastings 1891 (WSCC)

The opening of new hotels on Hastings seafront certainly helped change the tone of the town. The Queen's Hotel, opened in 1862 showed the way in taste and refinement, especially when it came to catering for the requirements of 'the ladies', as a contemporary newspaper report explained -

"The Queen's Hotel - for so it is named - has a principal front facing the sea, while from different parts of the building a great variety of views may be obtained. It is provided with a private entrance for families, and the ladies' coffee-room is one of the most elegant apartments ever devoted even to so worthy a purpose as to provide for the comfort of the lady visitors, without condemning them either to a solitary apartment or to the disorder of a common table. This splendid saloon is seventy feet long, and is divided by columns into four compartments, adorned with semicircular recesses. The entire room is lighted in the daytime by a succession of fine windows, those at the lower end facing the sea, and at night by four handsome crystal chandeliers, according admirably with the white and golden ornamentation, the green drapery and carpets, and the pillars and mantels of red marble. There are, in addition to this and the general coffee-room, twenty five private sitting-rooms (some of them combined with a sleeping alcove in the French fashion), dining, smoking, billiard, and bath rooms. One feature of resemblance to the great American hotels exists in the bridal apartments which are, of course, the most beautifully appointed."

Rye

With its timber-framed houses and cobbled streets, visitors to Rye could be forgiven for thinking they were in the middle of a film set for a 'costume drama'. The town is almost 'too good to be true'. It has an ancient gateway, a fine church with an ancient clock with performing figurines, an old stone fort, and an ambience which suggests that time has stood still here for several centuries, which in one sense at least is not untrue. Rye rose to prominence in the late medieval period, when it became a great export centre for the wool trade. By Tudor times it was one of the busiest ports in England. Everything seems to have been exported from here, the people of the town even traded their old shoes to the French. The high point in Rye's history came with the visit of Queen Elizabeth, who conferred the name 'Rye Royal' on the borough, and commended, "the noble entertainment she had, accompanied by the testimonies of love and loyalty, duty and reverence, she received from the people."

Victorian Rye (WSCC)

Rye had benefited from the silting up of the harbour at Winchelsea, but by the end of the sixteenth century its own harbour was suffering a similar fate. Without a harbour, Rye could not sustain the great wealth that had been generated in the previous century. The population, which at one time equalled or even exceeded that of Lewes and Chichester, now stagnated, and then declined. The leading families in the town were forced to cut their cloth accordingly. When their counter parts in the county towns were re-fronting or rebuilding their timber-framed houses in brick and stone during the eighteenth century, the burgesses of Rye had to make do with the old design. In other words the preservation of Tudor Rye is a testament to its subsequent decline. The town can be bitterly cold out of season, but that is the time to visit, for in the summer the throngs of tourists suffocate the spirit of old Rye. Best go in early November, when the residents are celebrating Bonfire Night, and the ghosts of Rye past making a fleeting visit on the present.

Bonfire Night is still a red letter day in much of Sussex, and particularly in this part of Sussex. It was once a night of wild, pagan celebration, when violence and disorder were only around the corner. Within living memory a burning boat was dragged through the streets every year on 'The Fifth'. The celebrations were often a rowdy affair, and as recently as fifty years ago, the piano from a hotel, whose proprietor had somehow 'offended' the locals, was dragged out of the premises, smashed up, and thrown onto the burning boat. Such conduct was common place in earlier times. In 1880 the Rye and District Chronicle reported that, "The proceedings were kept up until four o'clock on Saturday morning, about ten boats and seventy barrels having been burnt during the night. As nothing more could be found to destroy, the revellers gradually retired to change their apparel, and then departed home."

The last sentence hints at the elaborate disguises that were worn on such occasions, this, coupled with blackened faces ensured complete anonymity for the arsonists. The town authorities were powerless to act, and the small Rye police force could do nothing against hundreds of Bonfire Boys. When some prominent townsmen began to demand the suppression of the celebrations, the 'Boys' took their vengeance, as the South Eastern Advertiser for 1885 reported-

"There was a lull in proceedings about eleven o'clock. After the licensed houses were closed, a party of disguised men proceeded to Ferry-road, where they deliberately broke into an outbuilding which contained a valuable pleasure-boat, belonging to Mr. J. C. Vidler. It required a considerable amount of exertion to remove the craft, but the desperadoes at length succeeded, and a supply of inflammable material being forthcoming, she was soon alight, and was dragged to the centre of the adjoining bridge. Supt. Bourne, with the police and special constables, now offered some resistance, and prevented the party taking their plunder any further; but it was too late to save the boat, which was enveloped in flames, and was burnt through in several places. They therefore lifted what they could of the carcass, and dropped it into the river... We hear that Mr. Vidler has decided to offer a substantial reward in order that the thieves may be brought to justice, and there seems every reason to believe that this year's demonstration will again lead to magisterial investigation."

Only with the formal inclusion of Rye into the administrative county of East Sussex in 1889 did matters improve. From that year onwards, Rye came under the jurisdiction of the county police, and its Chief Constable, Major Luxford, who for many years felt it necessary to draft large numbers of constables into Rye every November 5, in order to prevent rioting and the destruction of property.

The Ypres Tower at Rye is named after William de Ypres, Earl of Kent, who had it built in 1162. It houses the town museum, including the gibbet chains of a notorious murderer (see p123) In Victorian times, and probably much earlier, local people pronounced the name as 'wipers', the same name given by English soldiers to the blood-stained Battle of Ypres in the First World War, which 'wiped out' a whole generation of young Englishmen.

Rye was a walled town with four 'gates', of which only the 'Landgate' survives today. Writing in 1894, Augustus Hare recalled that one gate had been lost to the sea, while two more had been pulled down in his own lifetime. He also noted that the town 'cucking' or ducking stool, the dread of all nagging and scolding women had only been destroyed in 1856.

Rye's history was for many years influenced by the large number of French Protestant refugees who settled in the town in the sixteenth and seventeenth centuries (see p75) Many surnames of French origin can still be found on the

Rye in 1891

old gravestones in the churchyard. In Mermaid Street, as well as the famous inn, there is also the home of the Jeake family, who chronicled the life of Rye over nearly one hundred years (see p75).

Winchelsea, although old and picturesque was once a 'new town' itself, and built to replace an earlier town lost to the sea. Eventually the new Winchelsea was stranded when the sea retreated, and now stands over a mile from the coast. The town is entered by one of two 'gates', which reinforce the sense of stepping back in time. Winchelsea made an impression of E V Lucas, who observed -

"It is important that the traveller who wishes to experience the right medieval thrill should come to Winchelsea either at dusk or at night. To make acquaintance with any new town by night is to double one's pleasure; for there is joy in the curious half-strangeness of the streets and houses, and a further joy in correcting by the morrow's light the distorted impression gathered in the dark. To come for the first time upon Winchelsea at dusk, whether from the station or from Rye, is to receive an impression almost if not quite unique in England; since there is no other town throned like this upon a green hill, to be gained only through massive gateways."

It was here that Wesley preached his last open-air sermon, and tried in vain to turn the local people away from a life of smuggling to one dedicated to Christ.

Brede is a quite unassuming village today, but it once had a reputation for rebellion. The notorious 'Swing' riots of 1830 in Sussex began at Brede (see p124) Brede Place was built during the reign of Henry VII, and was the home of the Oxenbridge family. During the Reformation of Henry VIII's reign (see p47), Sir Goddard Oxenbridge refused to turn away from the old religion, and became a hate figure for the Protestant zealots to be found in this part of Sussex. This probably explains how and why later generations turned Sir

Goddard into a child-eating giant. According to accounts written down in the nineteenth century, Sir Goddard was only killed when he was sawn in half at Groaning Bridge, the children of West Sussex taking one handle of the saw, the children of East Sussex, the other. Brede Place is another house notorious for its ghosts. A fire in 1979 gutted the building and may have frightened off the spooks as well.

Bodiam is justly famous for its castle, built in the late fourteenth century by Sir Edward Dalyngrige, a veteran of Crecy and Poitiers. It was slighted during the Civil War, and left as a ruin. Plans to demolish the castle entirely in 1829 were only forestalled by its purchase by John ('Mad Jack') Fuller of Brightling (see p124) In 1917 the castle was bought by Lord Curzon, who had it restored, and researched and wrote its history. When he died in 1926, Curzon left the castle to the National Trust. The bells in the church are dedicated to the Emperor Haile Selassie of Ethopia, who gave a generous donation towards the cost of having them made. The then vicar, the Rev. A. E. Cotton had been a military advisor to the Emperor during his war against Mussolini.

Battle is of course famous for being the site of the Battle of Hastings (see p29), it later became an important market town, dominated by the rich and powerful Battle Abbey (see pp47 and 51) From 1676 until 1874 there was a gunpowder industry at Battle, with workshops situated only a short distance from the Abbey. Little wonder then that the Bonfire Night celebrations at Battle were the noisiest in Sussex, and second only to Lewes for pageantry and show. For centuries a great bonfire burned opposite the Abbey gateway, however in recent years the 'Nanny State', in the guise of Sussex Police has intervened to stop this ancient tradition, and revellers have been diverted onto an out-of-town field. This author's great-grandfather was born in one of the small cottages close to the Abbey (an art gallery in 1998) on November 5 1850; his parents christened him 'Guy' - such was the Sussex enthusiasm for 'The Fifth'.

Bexhill may seem the poor relation of Hastings, but like its more famous neighbour, it too has an 'old town' and retains some historic buildings. The De La Warr's created Bexhill as a seaside resort after 1885. Bexhill scandalised polite society in 1898 by becoming the first resort in England to allow mixed sex bathing on its beaches. All the other Sussex resorts vowed not to follow Bexhill's 'French' inclinations, but within twenty years they had all succumbed. In 1978 the 136 million-year-old footprint of a Iguanodon, was found in mudstone on the seashore. The inventor of television, John Logie Baird died at Bexhill in 1946.

Battle in 1903 (FG)

THE VILLAGES OF THE HIGH WEALD

This most sparsely populated part of Sussex was once its most industrial area. From Crowborough down to Uckfield, and from Mayfield to Brightling, ironmasters employed hundreds, as did the wood industry, and its off-shoots, tanning and hurdle-making. Lime was burned, and gypsum mined. Glass was blown, and hops grown. For although Kent is always thought of as 'hops country', the eastern part of Sussex once had large 'gardens' as well. In 1881 it was estimated that up to 100,000 Londoners went to pick hops annually in Sussex and Kent, living in pickers camps for up to six weeks. In his book 'Sussex Industries', published in 1882, H. W. Wolf expressed the ambivalence of many Sussex people to the yearly migration from the capital -

"At a distance it is rather a pretty sight, passing by a hoppers' camp on an autumn evening, to watch the fires flaring in the dark, the tents pitched round, and the busy figures moving, the buzz of whose voices you can hear. It seems to suggest romance. But we must not go too near. At close quarters the eye pierces the poetic guise and detects an unsightly body."

Elsewhere in the book, Wolf gives us more details -

"Squatting together without very scrupulous regard to the laws of strict decency, drinking, and a free use of the English language not 'the Queen's', suit them to a T. And if on Saturday nights drunkenness leads to a free fight which makes 'terrified tradesmen cower behind their closed shutters', that is no more than what they look for and enjoy. Without this to them life might possibly appear not worth living. Prominent among these London hoppers are the Irish settlers, who come sometimes in shoals, and - freed from the influence of a supervising priest - appear to revel in wildness and fighting, once their blood is a little heated. They use their shillelaghs quite as deftly in Kent or Sussex as ever they could have done in old Erin."

At the time he was writing, Wolf says that the conduct of the pickers was improving, due in no small measure to the introduction of detached, brick-built shelters, and separate cooking houses, which were displacing the old tent encampments. The 'working holidays' to East Sussex and Kent continued up until the Second World War, and to a lesser extent up until the 1960's. Pickers also came down to gather in the apples from the large orchards which used to exist, although these were primarily in Kent. The increased popularity of foreign beers and foreign apples, coupled with automated methods of harvesting, have dramatically reduced the number of hop gardens and orchards, and eliminated the traditional exodus from London.

The iron industry came to an end at Ashburnham, when the last furnace closed in about 1812. The last worker at that forge died at Ashburnham in 1883. According to Sussex mythology the first forge in Sussex had been situated between Buxted and Mayfield, where according to a local ditty -

"Master Huggett and his man John,
They did cast the first cannon."

The iron industry in Sussex is discussed in more detail elsewhere in this book (see p66)

Crowborough is the highest town in Sussex. Its present-day respectability masks a wanton past. Writing in 1870, the antiquarian, M A Lower recalled that Crowborough had once been the most 'uncivilised' place in Sussex, and that the Warren had been, "a favourite resort for smugglers" (see p120) Richard Jefferies escaped to Crowborough in 1883, finding life in London unbearable, he wrote - "The dust of London fills the eyes and blurs the vision; but it penetrates deeper than that. There is the dust that chokes the spirit, and it is this that makes the streets so long, the stones so stony, the desk so wooden."

Jefferies, however was no idle romantic, he knew of the hardships of rural life, and once said of the countryside, "In real life I have remarked that it is frequently damp and rheumatic, and most hated by those who know it most." It was about the time that he was living at Crowborough that Jefferies wrote his essay, 'The Field Play/ Rural Dynamite' - a damning inditement of life in the poorer rural districts of England - such as the area around Crowborough.

Things must have improved considerably by 1907 however, the year that the esteemed novelist, Sir Arthur Conan Doyle came to live at Crowborough. Sir Arthur lived at 'Windlesham', and died there in 1930. Every year Crowborough celebrates the life and works of its most famous resident.

Uckfield was one of the Sussex iron towns, and the greatest ironmaster of them all, John Fuller, is buried in the parish church. A portrait to Fuller, who lived during the days of Queen Elizabeth, also hangs in the church, it shows

Uckfield Church (WSCC)

him dressed in the style of the religious puritans of his day - buttoned tunic and knee breeches. The solid iron memorial to Gabriel Egles was founded at the Fuller foundry in 1707. There is also a window in the church to a local Colonel who led a cavalry charge at Balaclava, during the Crimean War.

Uckfield is now a terminus for the railway, although the line used to carry on to Lewes, until the notorious 'Beeching Axe' fell in the 1960's. So neglected did Uckfield station become that it was still being lit by gas lamps until 1977. Not far from Uckfield is Nutley Windmill. The Mill ceased working before the First World War, and by 1970 it was in a terrible state of disrepair. It has however been fully restored by the Uckfield Preservation Society, which received a European Heritage Award for its efforts. Also saved in the 1970's was Uckfield House, which had been earmarked for demolition in 1972. The Heritage Museum is located at Bridge Cottage - a building dating back to the fourteenth century.

Heathfield is an old market town, once famous for its 'Cuckoo Fair', held every April 14, and so called because the first cuckoos were seen on this day. According to folklore an irascible old women let all the cuckoos out of her apron at Heathfield Fair, or 'Hefful Fair' as it would have been pronounced in the local dialect. Historically, Heathfield has long been associated with dissent, rebellion and non-conformity. The medieval rebel, Jack Cade (see p45) was run to ground near here and killed by Alexander Iden. The little village of **Cade Street** is named after the event. A large stone, still to be seen in the village, carries the following inscription -

"Near this spot was slain the notorious rebel Jack Cade by Alexander Iden, Sheriff of Kent, A.D. 1450. His body was carried to London and his head fixed upon London Bridge. This is the success of all rebels, and this fortune chanceth ever to traitors."

A traitor he may have been, but to local people he was a hero. As recently as the early 1960's, old farm workers in the district still recalled his name with pride, although they mistakenly identified him as being "one of Robin Hood's men." In Victorian times the road which led from Heathfield Common to Newick was still known as 'Iden's Way', and a mound close by was referred to as 'Jack Cade's Castle.'

During the sixteenth and seventeenth centuries, Heathfield was a stronghold of puritan values, and many of the names given to local children reflected this piety (see p74). During the Civil War, Heathfield rallied to the cause of Parliament. George Gilbert the militant Methodist minister built a chapel in the village, and died there at the age of 87 in 1827. Another famous resident was General George Elliott, who lived at Heathfield Park, then known as Heathfield Tower. He was famous for having seized, and then successfully held Gibraltar against the Spanish, a popular song of the day declared -

"When the Spaniards besiege`d Gibraltar, twas Elliott defended the place,

And he soon caused their plans for to alter, some died, others fled in disgrace."

In 1766 he was created Lord Heathfield, and was held to be one of the country's greatest military heroes - a reputation only surpassed by Nelson at Trafalgar in 1805.

The 'Vale of Heathfield' by the landscape painter, Turner, is regarded by some as the artist's best Sussex picture.

Religion features prominently in the history of **Mayfield**. It is said that in the early days of Christianity, St. Dunstan had a forge at Mayfield. Dunstan, who was tutor and spiritual guide to the young King Edgar, the first of the English kings to be anointed, is afforded by folklore the honour of tweaking the Devil's nose at Mayfield. According to the tale, the Devil was less than pleased with the good and peaceful state of England, and blamed Dunstan. So his Satanic Majesty disguised himself as a beautiful young woman, and set off to seduce the worthy Archbishop Dunstan. Dunstan, however was neither going to be tricked nor seduced, but recognised the Devil for who he was, and clamped the red-hot tongs from the forge onto the Devil's nose. Despite the flapping of his wings, the stamping of cloven hooves, and the cries of pain, Dunstan refused to let the Devil go until he promised never to torment the people of Sussex again. The Devil submitted, and flew off in great agony, only coming down to bathe his inflamed snout at a pool near Tunbridge Wells.

More factually, and more seriously, Mayfield was the scene of martyrdom to the Protestant cause during the reign of Mary (see p52)For over 130 years four generations of the Kirby family at Mayfield doubled up as both the religious and secular leaders of the village. They lived at a time when iron was king, and furnaces glowed brightly all around Mayfield. The old industry only survives today in local names, such as 'Cinder Hill' and 'Furnace Cottage.'

The Middle House gives the appearance of being an ancient English inn, and although the building dates back to the reign of Queen Elizabeth, and was built in the decade before the Armada set forth for these shores, it has only been an inn since the 1920's. It was said that a previous owner cruelly ill-used his wife, and kept her locked up for years in a small room in the roof space, just under one of the gables. This room still survives and is known as the 'prison chamber.' The Middle House has all the feel of an inn of the old days - the accommodation is basic, but the breakfasts are big and hearty. Too often modern hotels lavish guests with comfort while skimping on the eggs and bacon!

The Mayfield smugglers of the eighteenth century were almost as notorious as their near neighbours at Hawkhurst (see p121). The tombs in the churchyard are supposed to have been used for the storage of contraband.

Rudyard Kipling finally found peace and quiet when he moved from Rottingdean to Burwash in 1902. The great poet ended his days at Batemans, the old manor house. From here he penned many verses with a Sussex flavour, including 'Puck's Song', which alludes to the history and traditions of this part of the county -

See you the ferny ride that steals
Into the oak-woods far?
O that was whence they hewed the keels
That rolled to Trafalgar.

And mark you where the ivy clings
To Bayham's mouldering walls?
O there we cast the stout railings
That stand around St. Pauls.

See you the dimpled track that runs
All hollow through the wheat?
O that was where they hauled the guns
That smote King Philip's fleet.

(Out of the Weald, the secret Weald,
Men sent in ancient years
The horse-shoes red at Flodden Field,
The arrows at Poitiers!)

See you our little mill that clacks,
So busy by the brook?
She has ground her corn and paid her tax
Ever since Domesday Book.

See you our stilly woods of oak,
And the dread ditch beside?
O that was where the Saxons broke
On the day that Harold died.

Kipling was arguably the most famous and most popular man of his day. Not since Shakespeare had ordinary people, as well the wealthy and the educated, enjoyed and appreciated contemporary literature. Kipling had influence at the highest levels, he had the ear of the King, and in 1923 his cousin, Stanley Baldwin became Prime Minister. Moving in literary and academic circles could prove wearisome, and Kipling therefore appreciated the uncomplicated, uncluttered logic of the country people. One old man told him that the key to a happy life was to, "Keep your feet warm, your head cool, eat onions and do not think too deeply." George V was the last British king to bear the title 'Emperor', it was, therefore, that Rudyard Kipling, the chronicler of the Empire should die on the same day as his Imperial Majesty - 18 January 1936.

Burwash's main street, with its weather-boarded cottages, and indomitable old houses seems to retain a spirit of those elusive 'olden times', which of course really only exists in our dreams. In reality the village was once very poor, and times remained harsh until well into the nineteenth century (see p126)

Brightling was the home of John Fuller (1757-1834), known as 'Mad Jack'. His desire to help the poor of his own day, and to be remembered by future generations, compelled him to embark on some very maverick building schemes. These projects gave employment to local men at a time when wages were low and unemployment was high. The Observatory and the Rotunda are sane enough for the time in which they were built (early nineteenth century), the Tower is in the genre of many other Regency follies, while the 'Obelisk' or 'Brightling Needle' as it is often called was built to mark Wellington's victory at Waterloo. The 'Sugar Loaf' is however true eccentricity, and is supposed to have been built in an effort to fool Fuller's friends into believing that the spire of Brightling church (which it closely resembles) could be seen from the grounds of Fuller's home.

Touring around Brightling, looking for Fuller's Follies is a day's excursion in itself. In Brightling churchyard can be found the last of the Squire's monuments - the stone pyramid in which he is buried. Another lasting epitaph to Fuller is Bodiam Castle, which he purchased in order to preserve it from

Bodiam Castle (WSCC)

demolition. A century later it was given to the nation by Lord Curzon, who had undertaken its renovation: but had it not been for Fuller, this castle, arguably the finest in Sussex, would have been lost. The life of this exceptional man is well documented in Geoff Hutchinson's book, *Fuller of Sussex – A Georgian squire.*

Hilaire Belloc, who resembled Fuller, both in girth and personality, devoted several paragraphs of his book, 'The Four Men' to the story of how Fuller, a Member of the House of Commons was expelled for insulting both the Speaker and the House. Belloc was for a time an MP himself, and like Fuller became wholly disillusioned with the place. The following extract, brimming with literary license, tells us as much about Belloc as it does about Fuller -

" Well then, when he had come to Westminster, very soon there was a day in which the Big-wigs would have a debate, all empty and worthless, upon Hot Air, or the value of nothingness; and the man who took most money there out of the taxes, and his first cousin who sat opposite and to whom he had promised the next wad of public wealth, and his brother-in-law and his parasite and all

Hilaire Belloc

the rest of the thieves had begun their pompous folly, when great Fuller arose in his place, full of the South, and said that he had not come to the Commons House to talk any such balderdash, or to hear it, but contrariwise proposed, then and there, to give them an Eulogy upon the County of Sussex, from which he had come and which was the captain ground and head county of the whole world."

" This Eulogy he very promptly and powerfully began, using his voice as a healthy man should, who will drown all opposition and who can call a dog to heel from half a mile away. And indeed though a storm rose round him from all those lesser men, who had come to Westminster, not for the praise and honour of their land, but to fill their pockets, he very manfully shouted and was heard above it all, so that the Sergeant-at-Arms grew sick with fear, and the Clerk at the Table wished he had never been born. But the Speaker, whose business it is to keep the place inane (I do not remember his name, for such men are not famous after death), stood up in his gown and called to Fuller that he was out of order. And since Fuller would not yield, every man in the house called out 'Order!' eight or nine hundred times. But when they were exhausted, the great Fuller, Fuller of Brightling, cried out over them all:

'Do you think I care for you, you insignificant little man in the wig? Take that!" And with these words he snapped his fingers in the face of the bunch of them, and walked out of the Commons House, and got into his great coach with its six powerful horses, and ordering their heads to be set southwards he at last regained his own land, where he was received as such a man should be, with bells ringing and guns firing, little boys cheering, and all ducks, hens, and pigs flying from before his approach to the left and to the right of the road. Ever since that day it has been held a singular honour and one surpassing all others to be a squire of Brightling, but no honour whatsoever to be a member of the Commons House. He spent all his great fortune upon the poor of Sussex and of his own parish, bidding them drink deep and eat hearty as being the habits the best preservative of life, until at last he also died. There is the story of Fuller of Brightling, and may we all deserve as well as he."

Bibliography/ Further Reading

Dear Amberley, Rev. E Noel Staines (self-published 1968)

Arundel - A History of the Town and Castle, Joseph H Preston
(Associated University Press 1993)

Arundel Castle, John Martin Robinson (Phillimore 1994)

Arundel - A Guide, Harold Evans (Evans & Sons 1995)

The Mill & The Murrell, Barnham, Mervyn Cutten & Vic May (Mervyn Cutten 1992)

Beachy Head, John Surtees (SB Publicatiobs 1997)

Battle, Rye & the villages, Geoff Hutchinson (self-published, undated)

The Chronicle of Battle Abbey, translated by Eleanor Searle (Clarendon Press 1980)

Bygone Battle, Aylwin Guilmant (Phillimore 1983)

The Story of Bexhill, L J Bartley (F J Parsons Ltd. 1971)

A History of Bognor Regis, Gerard Young (Phillimore 1983)

Bodiam Castle (National Trust 1991)

Brighton Town and Brighton People, Antony Dale (Phillimore1976)

Life in Brighton, Clifford Musgrave (Faber & Faber 1970)

Brighton, Old Ocean's Bauble, Edmund M Gilbert (Flare Books 1975)

Burgess Hill, Hugh Matthews (Phillimore 1989)

Restricted Grandeur - Impressions of Chichester 1586-1948, Timothy J McCann
(WSCC 1995)

Chichester - A Documentary History, Roy Morgan (Phillimore 1992)

Chichester Cathedral - An Historical Survey, (Ed. Mary Hobbs) (Phillimore 1994)

A History of Crawley, Peter Gwynne (Phillimore 1990)

Crowborough - The Growth of a Wealden Town, Malcolm R Payne (
K A F Brewen Books, 1985)

A Chronicle of Cuckfield, Maisie Wright (Cuckfield Musuem Trust 1991)

Eastbourne - A Pictorial History, D Robert Elleray (Phillimore 1995)

Around East Grinstead, David Gould (Sutton Publishing Ltd 1997)

Hailsham and its Environs, Charles A Robertson (Phillimore 1982)

Hastings - A living History, David William Thornton (Hastings Publishing Co. 1987)

Historic Hastings, J Manwaring Baines (P F J Parsons 1955)

Fishermen of Hastings, Steve Peake (Newsbooks 1985)

The Metropolis of Mid-Sussex - A History of Haywards Heath, Wyn K Ford & A C
Gabe (Charles Clarke 1981)

Heathfield Park - A private estate and a wealden town, Roy Pryce
(self-published 1996)

Horsham Houses, Annabelle Hughes (Phillimore 1986)

Horsham & District, Tony Wales (Alan Sutton 1994)

A History of Hove, Judy Middleton (Phillimore 1979)

Georgian Lewes, Colin Brent (Colin Brent Books 1993)

Unknown Lewes, John Houghton (Tartarus Press 1997)

Littlehampton - A Pictorial History, D Robert Elleray (Phillimore 1991)

Mayfield - The Story of a Wealden Village, E M Bell-Irving (Republished by ESCC 1984)

Midhurst - A Brief History, Francis Johnston-Davies (Midhurst Society 1996)

Petworth House (National Trust 1997)

Tread Lightly Here - An affectionate look at Petworth's ancient streets, Peter Jerome (Window Press 1990)

Tudor Rye, Graham Mayhew (CCE 1987)

A Maritime History of Rye, John Collard (John Collard 1985)

Bygone Seaford, John Odam (Phillimore 1990)

A History of Selsey, Frances Mee (Phillimore 1988)

A Walkabout Guide to Shoreham, Micheal Norman (Marlipins Museum 1984)

Slindon - A Portrait of a Sussex Village, J Duggan-Rees (self-published 1988)

Bygone Steyning, Bramber and Beeding, Alwyn Guilmant (Phillimore 1988)

Around Uckfield, Uckfield & District Preservation Society (Chalford 1997)

Wivelsfield - The History of a Wealden Parish ,Ed. Heather Warne (Pier Point Publishing 1994)

Historic Worthing - the untold story, Chris Hare (Windrush 1991)

The Saxon and Norman Heritage

The South-East to AD 1000, Peter Drewitt, David Rudling, Mark Gardiner (Longman 1988)

The South-East from AD 1000, Peter Brandon & Brian Short (Longman 1990)

The Archaeology of Sussex, E Cecil Curwen (Methuen 1954)

The English Settlements, J N L Myers (Oxford University Press 1989)

The Anglo-Saxon Chronicle, translated and collated by Anne Savage (Heinemann 1983)

Anglo-Saxon England, Sir Frank Stenton (Oxford University Press 1989)

The Reformation

Religion and Society in Elizabethan Sussex, Roger B Manning (Leicester University Press 1969)

The Friars in Sussex, 1228-1928, E B Poland (Combridges 1928)

Studies in Sussex Church History, Ed. M J Kitch (leopard's Head Press 1981)

The South Saxon See and the Cathedral Church of Chichester, Rev. W R W Stephens (Richard Bentley & Sons 1876)

The English Reformation, A G Dickens (Fontana 1967)

The Civil War

Sussex 1600-1660 - A County Community in Peace and War, Anthony J Fletcher (Longman 1975)

Sussex in the Great Civil War and the Interegnum 1642-1660, Thomas Staford
(Chiswick 1910)
The Civil War and Mid 17th-Century Chichester (Chichester District Museum 1992)
Revel, Riot & Rebellion - Popular Culture in England 1603-1660, David Underman
(Oxford University Press 1987)
The English Revolution, Barry Coward and Chris Durston (John Murray 1998)

Crime and Punishment
The Diary of Thomas Turner 1754-1765, Ed. David Vaisey (CTR Publishing 1994)
A Millenium of Facts in the History of Horsham and Sussex, 947-1947, William
Albery (1947)
The Hanging Tree - Execution & the English People, V A C Gatrell (Oxford
University Press 1996)
Captain Swing, Eric Hobsbawn and George Rude (Lawrence Wishart 1969)
Social Protest in Rural Society, Andrew Charlesworth (Univeristy of Liverpool 1979)

General Books
The South Downs, Dr. Peter Brandon (Phillimore 1998)
The Downland Shepherd, Shaun Payne & others (Alan Sutton) 1989
A Short History of Sussex, John Lowerson (W. Dawson and Son 1980)
A History of Sussex, J R Armstrong (Phillimore 1995)
A History of the Sussex People - Chris Hare (Southern Heritage 1995)
Castles in Sussex, John Guy (Phillimore 1984)
The Folklore of Sussex, Jacqueline Simpson (Batsford 1972)
Sussex Industrial Archaeology - a field guide, eds. B Austen, D Cox, J Upton
(Phillimore 1985)
A Sussex Garland, Tony Wales (Countryside Books 1986)
Bob Copper's Sussex, Bob Copper (SB Publications 1997)
The Buildings of England - Sussex, Ian Nairn & Nicholas Pevsner (Penguin 1985)
Smuggling in Kent & Sussex 1700 - 1840, Mary Waugh (Countryside Books 1985)
Smuggling - The Wicked Trade, John Douch (Crabwell Publications 1980)
The English Rural Community Image & Analysis, Ed.
(Cambridge University Press 1992)
Writers on the Coast, Ed. Eric Bird & Lilian James (Windrush 1992)
Writers in Sussex, Bernard Smith & Peter Haas (Redcliffe 1985)
West Sussex - Literary, Musical & Artistic Links (WSCC 1993)

*Any reader with an inquiry regarding a specific reference should telephone the author on
(01903) 532681 or (01903) 695612. Please do not write to the author requesting such
information.*

Place-names Index

Literary Index

THE
HASTINGS
SCHOOL
ACADEMY
1848

THE HASTINGS ACADEMY

SCHOOL LIBRARY

Rye Road, Hastings, East Sussex, TN35 5DN